BICYCLING®
MAGAZINE'S

Complete Book of

ROAD CYCLING

Skills

Your Guide to Riding Faster,
Stronger, Longer, and Safer

By Ed Pavelka and the
Editors of **BICYCLING**
MAGAZINE

RODALE

Notice

The information in this book is meant to supplement, not replace, proper road cycling training. Like any sport involving speed, equipment, balance, and environmental factors, road cycling poses some inherent risk. The editors and publisher advise readers to take full responsibility for their safety and know their limits. Before practicing the skills described in this book, be sure that your equipment is well-maintained, and do not take risks beyond your level of experience, aptitude, training, and comfort level.

Copyright © 1998 by Rodale Inc.
Cover photograph copyright © 1998 by John Kelly

Printed in the United States of America
Rodale Inc. makes every effort to use acid-free ∞, recycled paper ♺.

Library of Congress Cataloging-in-Publication Data

Pavelka, Ed.
    Bicycling magazine's complete book of road cycling skills : your guide to riding faster, stronger, longer, and safer / by Ed Pavelka and the editors of Bicycling magazine.
      p.   cm.
    Includes index.
    ISBN-13 978–0–87596–486–7 paperback
    ISBN-10 0–87596–486–9 paperback
    1. Bicycle racing—Training.   I. Bicycling magazine.   II. Title.
GV1048.P38   1998
796.6′2—dc21   97–33429

Distributed to the trade by Holtzbrinck Publishers

    16 18 20 19 17 15   paperback

WE **INSPIRE** AND **ENABLE** PEOPLE TO IMPROVE
THEIR LIVES AND THE WORLD AROUND THEM

FOR MORE OF OUR PRODUCTS
WWW.**RODALESTORE**.COM
(800) 848-4735

Bicycling Magazine's Complete Book of Road Cycling Skills

Editorial Staff

Executive Director, New Ventures, *Bicycling* Magazine: Ed Pavelka

Editor: John D. Reeser

Writers: John Allen; Arnie Baker, M.D.; Edmund R. Burke, Ph.D.; Geoff Drake; Jim Langley; Gary Legwold; Fred Matheny; Michael McGettigan; Rory O'Reilly; Jo Ostgarden; Robert M. Otto, Ph.D.; Ed Pavelka; Nelson Pena; Davis Phinney; Julie Walsh

Copy Editors: Linda Mooney, Karen Neely

Associate Art Director: Charles Beasley

Cover Designer: Charles Beasley

Cover Photographer: John Kelly

Book Designer: Stan Green/Green Graphics

Interior Illustrators: J. Andrew Brubaker, John Karapelou

Layout Designer: Andrew MacBride

Manufacturing Coordinator: Melinda B. Rizzo

Office Manager: Roberta Mulliner

Office Staff: Julie Kehs, Mary Lou Stephen

Editorial Assistant, *Bicycling* Magazine: Chris Engleman

Rodale Health and Fitness Books

Vice-President and Editorial Director: Debora T. Yost

Executive Editor: Neil Wertheimer

Design and Production Director: Michael Ward

Research Manager: Ann Gossy Yermish

Copy Manager: Lisa D. Andruscavage

Book Manufacturing Director: Helen Clogston

C O N T

E N T S

INTRODUCTION

Almost two decades ago, I became friends with a man who was having an historic impact on American cycling. His name is Eddie Borysewicz, but for obvious reasons he became known to everyone as Eddie B. This coach from Poland brought something that turned the table for the U.S. national team: a no-nonsense approach based on his inside knowledge of how the dominant Europeans trained and raced. The results were spectacular. Six years after Eddie took charge of U.S. road and track racing, American riders won nine medals in the 1984 Olympics—their best showing since the turn of the century. Davis Phinney, a contributor to this book, was one of Eddie's stars.

Just before that medal haul, Eddie and I collaborated on a book called *Bicycle Road Racing*, his complete program for training and competition. I still remember the hours we spent discussing its content. For a week, Eddie carefully explained everything into my tape recorder. He spoke broken English then, making it tough for me to use anything verbatim, but his enthusiasm was unmistakable. One thing above all still sticks in my mind. In discussing what it takes to be a good cyclist, Eddie said it begins with one basic trait. "First," he said, "you must love the exercise of riding a bike."

I can assure you that Davis Phinney and each of the contributors to this book pass Eddie's test. What you're holding is our way of helping you love riding, too. From our various areas of expertise, we provide the full range of road riding advice—training, tactics, equipment, nutrition, bike-handling skills, and even a unique section on how to ride safely and confidently in traffic. Our tips on indoor cycling, off-season conditioning, and winter riding will help you enjoy cycling's benefits all year round. To top it off, we include information about two types of bicycles, tandems and recumbents, that can add fun and diversity to your cycling experience. Give 'em a try!

Whatever your goals in road riding, you now have the best advice from the sport's best writers. To learn even more and stay current with cycling's opportunities and technology, I also invite you to read *Bicycling* magazine, available monthly at your favorite bike shop or newsstand. See you on the road!

Ed Pavelka
Executive Director
Bicycling Magazine's New Ventures

The Basics

A PERFECT POSITION

By Geoff Drake

To get the most out of cycling, make sure your bike fits your body and follow some simple position pointers. By doing so you'll enjoy riding more because you'll have fewer pains and strains. You'll also have greater strength and endurance. It's easy—just do the following steps and make changes, as necessary. But if you have been riding for a while and your position needs a significant adjustment, make the change little by little over several weeks to avoid injury. And remember, these are only guidelines. If you feel better with some positions slightly outside these norms, that's fine. (For more information on women's concerns regarding bike fit, see chapter 43.)

1. Arms. Beware road rider's rigor mortis. Keep your elbows bent and relaxed to absorb shock and prevent veering when you hit a bump. Keep your arms in line with your body, not splayed to the side, to make a more compact, aerodynamic package.

2. Upper body/shoulders. Two operative words: Be still. Imagine the calories burned by rocking side to side with every pedal stroke on a 25-mile ride. You're better off using that energy for pedaling. Also, beware of creeping forward on the saddle and hunching your back when tired. Shift to a higher gear and stand to pedal periodically to relieve saddle pressure and prevent stiffness in your hips and back.

3. Head and neck. There is nothing more embarrassing—or dangerous—than riding into the rear of a parked car. So avoid putting your head down, especially when you're tired. Periodically tilt your head side to side to stretch and relax the neck muscles.

4. Hands. With your hands on the bar tops, imagine that your fingers are so loose that you could play the piano. A white-knuckle hold on the bar is unnecessary and will produce energy-sapping muscle tension throughout the arms and shoulders. Grasp the drops for descents or high-speed riding and the brake hoods for relaxed cruising. On long climbs hold the top of the bar to sit upright and to open the chest for easier breathing. Wear padded gloves and change hand position frequently to prevent finger numbness and upper-body stiffness. When standing, grasp the brake hoods lightly, and gently rock the bike side to side in sync with your pedal strokes. Always keep each thumb and a finger closed around the hood or bar to prevent losing hold on an unexpected bump.

5. Handlebar. Bar width should equal shoulder width. (Bars are commonly available in 38-, 40-, and 42-centimeter sizes.) Err on the side of a wider one to open your chest for breathing. Some models are available with a large drop (vertical distance) to help big hands fit into the hooks. Position the flat bottom portion of the bar horizontal or pointed slightly down toward the rear hub.

6. Brake levers. You can move the levers up or down the curve of the bar for comfort. They're usually set so that each lever tip touches a straightedge extended forward from under the flat bottom portion of

A low, balanced position increases speed while reducing strain.

the bar. To move the lever, peel back its hood to find the clamp bolt. It may be on the side, or inside when you hold down the handle.

7. Stem height. With your stem high enough (normally about an inch below the top of the saddle), you'll be more inclined to use the drops. Putting it lower can improve aerodynamics, but you may be less comfortable and not take advantage of that. Never position the stem where its maximum extension line shows above the headset. Your force on the bar could break the stem.

8. Top tube and stem extension. These combined dimensions, which determine your "reach," vary according to your flexibility and anatomy. There is no ultimate prescription, but there is a good starting point: When you are comfortably seated with elbows slightly bent and hands on the brake hoods, the front hub should be obscured by the handlebar. If the hub appears in front of the bar or behind it, consider replacing the stem with one of appropriate extension. As you gain experience, you may benefit from a longer extension to improve aerodynamics and flatten your back.

9. Back. A flat back is the defining mark of a pro rider. The correct stem and top-tube combination is crucial for this, but so is hip flexibility. Concentrate on rotating the top of your hips forward. If you think of trying to touch the top tube with your stomach, it will help stop you from rounding your back.

10. Saddle height. There are various formulas for this, but you don't have to be a mathematician to know what the correct height looks like. Your knees should be slightly bent at the bottom of the pedal stroke, and when viewed from behind, your hips shouldn't rock on the saddle. Try this quick method that is used at the Olympic Training Center: Have someone set the height so there are 5 millimeters of clearance between your heel and the pedal at the bottom of the stroke. (Add a few millimeters if you use a clipless pedal system or if your shoes have very thin soles at the heel compared to the forefoot. Also, raise the saddle 2 to 3 millimeters if you have long feet for your height.) For those who have knee pain caused by chondromalacia, a saddle on the higher side of the acceptable range can be therapeutic, so gradually raise it until hip rocking begins, then lower it slightly. Make saddle height changes 2 millimeters at a time to avoid strain.

11. Saddle tilt. The saddle should be level, which you can check by laying a straightedge along its length. A slight downward tilt may be more comfortable if you're using an extreme forward position with an aero bar and elbow rests, but too much tilt causes you to slide forward and place additional weight on your arms.

12. Fore/aft saddle position. When you're seated comfortably in the center of the saddle with the crankarms horizontal, get someone to drop a plumb line from the front of your forward kneecap. It should touch the end of the crankarm. This is the neutral position, and you should be able to achieve it by loosening the seat clamp and sliding the saddle fore or aft. (Be sure to recheck the tilt before retightening.) Climbers, time trialists, and some road racers prefer the line to fall a couple of centimeters behind the end of the crankarm to increase leverage in big gears. Conversely, track and criterium racers like a more forward position to improve leg speed. Remember, if your reach to the handlebar is wrong, use the stem extension to correct it, not fore/aft saddle position.

13. Frame. Don't succumb to big-bike syndrome. In general, smaller frames are lighter and stiffer. Have someone measure your inseam from crotch to floor, with bare feet 6 inches apart, and multiply by 0.65. This equals your road-frame size, measured along the seat tube from the center of the bolt that attaches the crankarm to the bike to the center of the top tube. As a double check, this should produce 4 to 5 inches of exposed seatpost when your saddle height is correct. (The post's maximum extension line shouldn't show. If it does, purchase a longer post.)

14. Butt. By sliding rearward or forward on the saddle, you can emphasize different muscle groups. This can be useful on a long climb. Moving forward emphasizes the quadriceps muscle on the front of the thigh, while moving backward accentuates the opposite side, the hamstrings. Sitting in different locations also relieves the constant pressure that may cause genital numbness.

15. Feet. Think of your footprints as you walk from a swimming pool. Some of us are pigeon-toed and others are duck-footed. To prevent knee injury, strive for a cleat position that accommodates your natural foot angle. Make cleat adjustments on rides until you feel comfortable, or pay a shop to do it with the Rotational Adjustment Device, which is part of the Fit Kit bicycle sizing system. Better still, use a clipless pedal system that allows your feet to pivot freely ("float"), thus making precise adjustment unnecessary. Position cleats fore and aft so that the widest part of each foot is over the pedal axle.

16. Pedaling technique. Visualize scraping mud from the underside of your shoe at the bottom of each stroke. This helps eliminate dead spots where no force is being applied. Try to lift on the backstroke to reduce the negative (downward) weight that studies say most riders inadvertently apply.

17. Crankarm length. The trend is toward longer crankarms, which add power but may inhibit pedaling speed. In general, if your inseam is less than 29 inches, use 165-millimeter crankarms; 29 to 32 inches, 170-millimeter; 33 to 34 inches, 172.5-millimeter; and more than 34 inches, 175-millimeter. Crankarm length is measured from the center of the fixing bolt to the center of the pedal mounting hole. It's usually stamped on the back of the arm.

GET A GRIP

By Geoff Drake

While your legs supply the locomotion, your hands provide a critical contact point for climbing, sprinting, and flatland riding. Each situation requires a different grip for efficiency and comfort. Fortunately, the common drop bar provides an elegant, simple solution, offering six basic positions and infinite variations. Switch often to prevent nerve compression, which causes numbness and hand fatigue, and always keep two fingers closed around the bar or brake hoods to prevent losing control on bumps. Wear padded gloves for comfort and to avoid abrasions in a fall.

1. Both hands on top. Use this grip for sustained seated climbing or when pushing hard at slower speeds. In these instances the ability to open the chest and breathe freely is more important than aerodynamic efficiency. Because braking is impossible with this grip, don't follow others too closely or use this grip when riding in a pack.

Grasp the bar about 2 inches from either side of the stem. A narrower grip sacrifices leverage and control, while a wider one splays the elbows and creates drag. Keep your wrists and elbows slightly bent. Hold the bar lightly, but don't forget to keep at least two fingers closed around it. For added power, pull with one arm while pushing with the opposite leg, then relax that arm. Greg LeMond favored this technique on steep climbs, rocking powerfully from side to side.

2. One hand on top. When removing a hand to eat, drink, or stretch, place the other hand an inch from the stem. This is the safest position because oversteering is less likely when the hand is close to the turning axis. Look at the road ahead first to ensure that the pavement is smooth and that your hand won't be jarred loose. Don't use

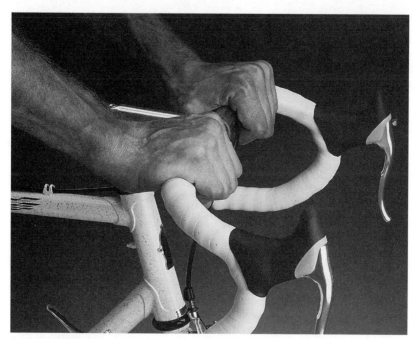

Both hands on top.

this position when riding in a pack unless you're sitting up to refuel at the rear.

3. On the hoods. Like your favorite sofa, this is where you go to relax. It's more aerodynamic than riding on the tops but still offers easy breathing. Use it for flatland cruising or when riding in a pack. (Don't use it, however, when trying to ride fast or against the wind. Even when drafting, the aerodynamic cost is too great.) It's also the best position for out-of-saddle climbing.

Place the thumbs to the inside of the hoods and rest one or two fingers on the levers for quick braking. Rest the center of your palms on the bar's upper curves. Keep your elbows bent but not flared outward. When standing, close two fingers around the hoods for a firmer grip.

To prevent cocking the wrists excessively, make sure the levers are correctly positioned. Here's the rule: A straightedge extended from under the flat lower portion of the bar should touch the tip of the lever. This bottom part of the bar should be horizontal or pointed a few degrees down toward the rear hub.

For an aero alternative to riding the drops (position 5), hold the hoods and bend your arms 90 degrees. Lower your chin toward the stem and try to achieve a flat back. This position, favored by Eddy

Merckx and other top pros, keeps you low while still allowing your shoulders and arms to relax.

4. On the hoods/fingers split. This variation of position 3 is an excellent way to relieve pressure from the normal weight-bearing part of the palms. It also facilitates bending the elbows to achieve a low aero position. It makes braking impossible, however, so don't use it in a pack.

Place your index fingers to the inside of the hoods and rest the center of your palms on the bar's upper curves. (Or you may prefer Mr. Spock's "live long and prosper" technique, placing two fingers on either side of the hoods.) Lightly close each thumb and one other finger around the bar. This position allows a relatively low aero position. It's a refreshing diversion, but switch to another grip before the hood peaks press in at the bottom of your split fingers.

5. On the drops. This is what drop bars were made for, and it's the most aerodynamic position for fast flatland riding and descending. It's also good for short, powerful, out-of-saddle efforts such as sprinting or surmounting small hills. Most riders find that it's not comfortable for long, however, and that it doesn't provide much climbing leverage.

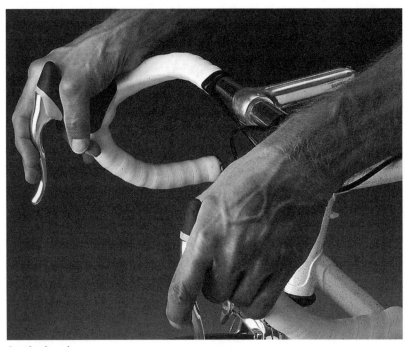

On the hoods.

On the drops.

Use it at least a few times on every ride to develop the necessary flexibility and arm strength.

Rest the edge of your hands (below the pinkie) on the flat portion of the bar with your wrists straight. Keep your elbows bent and in line with your body. When riding in a pack, descending, or cornering, keep one or two fingers on the levers for quick braking. During hard solo efforts, bend your arms more to get lower, but keep your head up.

Hand size can be accommodated by bars with different drops (the distance from the center of the bar top to the center of the flat bottom portion). A large drop is 16 centimeters; normal, 15 centimeters; shallow, 14 centimeters.

6. On the bottom. This provides the same aero advantage as position 5 but offers a different grasp to alleviate hand numbness. It also allows you to reach bar-end shifters with minimal movement. Disadvantages are that you must move to use the brakes, and your wrists can fatigue because they are cocked. Keep your elbows in. To become more aero, bend your arms 90 degrees.

This position has one other use: time trial starts. Firmly grasp the handlebar, palms up, lock your arms, and push and pull with a rigid upper body to get maximum acceleration off the line.

Pedal the Right Way to
Save Energy and Boost Speed

SMOOTH SPINNING

By Davis Phinney

Great cyclists make even the hardest rides look easy. In fact, while winning five Tour de France races, Miguel Indurain was criticized for making it look too easy. How did he do that? Natural ability, sure. Lots of miles, absolutely.

How you pedal affects your style on the bike. The smoother you can power the drivetrain, the more relaxed and stable your upper body becomes—like Indurain. The more motion there is in your upper body, the sloppier your pedaling will be.

The fact is, pedaling is an art, maybe even a lost art. It's the most basic element of our sport. You used to see packs of wool-clad cyclists emulating the Europeans by doing early-season, low-gear miles. The idea was to develop form first, speed second. In winter they rode rollers, which also put a premium on pedaling style and helped develop balance. (With rollers, a lapse in concentration or uneven, erratic pedaling can put a cyclist in a heap on the floor. Contrast this to the stationary trainer, on which a rider can have terrible form or even pick up bad habits.)

In an earlier era *souplesse* was a term often heard in describing a smooth, stylish rider. High-revolution-per-minute miles were a rite of passage, and all racing was done on tracks with fixed-gear bikes. Pedaling style was a priority. As cycling evolved in the United States, the tenet of "spin into form" fell away. The modern-day road ride is a big-ring hammerfest, where style and form disappear as riders start getting blown off the back when the action heats up.

But even today, the smoothest riders have a track background. My former teammate, Frankie Andreu, is one such rider. Although lacking the bionic strength of a Lance Armstrong, he continues to improve his physical capacity, so his results get better each year. Having refined his style on the track early in his career, he was able to focus on road training without having to correct bad habits along the way. That was always one advantage of the old school.

POWERFUL PEDALING

Even the best cyclists can benefit from enhancing pedal dynamics. Lance Armstrong is a case in point. He has a very fit body and his results speak volumes (1993 world champion and a Tour de France stage winner). But the good athlete always looks for improvement, and Armstrong's pedaling technique was in need of upgrading.

In the 1993 Tour DuPont his battle with eventual winner Raul Alcala was a study in contrast. In the final stage time trial, Alcala had made up a 2-minute deficit early and smoothly rode past the laboring Armstrong. While Armstrong thrashed, Alcala pedaled with an elegant smoothness that defied the effort. The style masters always make it look easy.

Taking note of this weakness in his rising star, coach Chris Carmichael prescribed two drills for Armstrong: one-legged pedaling and fixed-gear riding, which is the old-school method of improving spin. Here's how both methods work.

One-legged pedaling. This is best done indoors where you can ride on a trainer and put your nonpedaling leg up on a box or stool. It forces you to pedal all the way through the stroke and develop your muscles accordingly. Make it a regular feature of your off-season stationary workouts. Start with just 20 revolutions and increase this to several minutes at a stretch, two to five times per workout for each leg. I do this in a 53 × 16-tooth (53 × 16T) gear, but you should determine what is comfortable on the resistance on your trainer.

Fixed-gear riding. A fixed-gear bike is like the tricycle you rode as a child—if the bike is moving, the pedals are going around. No coasting. And that's the magic. Because you are stuck in one gear, you must smooth your stroke or get bounced around like a basketball, especially on the downhills. Armstrong used a fairly small gear (42 × 17T) in order to hone his spin. Installing a fixed gear requires special (but inexpensive) equipment. Ask your local shop to help you set it up.

The old-school rider would use a fixed gear for the first 1,000 miles of each season, forcing the muscles to remember that nice, round pedal stroke and prohibiting the use of big gears until a good base was developed. (One caution: Fixed-gear riding isn't suitable for hilly terrain. Because you can't gear down when climbing, it puts undue stress on the knees. On descents it might result in excessive braking to control the fast cadence.)

Other methods. You can also improve your spin by riding in a small gear and pedaling all the downhills. Do this once or twice a week. It requires strong discipline to keep up with the gear so that you're pedaling at a very high revolution-per-minute rate—up to 150. At first you may feel as if you'll bounce right out of your cleats. Relax. Spin. With time your pedal stroke will become smooth.

Although studies have shown that you can't actually apply a positive force on the upstroke, it's important to at least have the perception of constant pressure all the way around. You can also have a coach watch you pedal, or install a mirror next to your indoor trainer and critique yourself.

MINIMIZE MOVEMENT

It's good practice to keep your upper body as motionless as possible. One good exercise involves riding up a long, gradual hill (5 percent grade) in a big gear (53 × 15T is what I use). At first, ride for only a minute or so, then build up to several 5-minute repetitions per workout. Strive for as little motion and arm action as possible and stay in the saddle. This, like one-legged pedaling, gives you a feel for a complete, round stroke. It's like weight lifting on the bike. Be forewarned: It's not suitable for anyone with bad knees, and it can lead to poor habits if done to the point of sloppiness (when you start twisting and lurching). Don't try it unless you have a good fitness base.

Improving your pedal stroke should be an important part of the technical work in your training program. Use the drills I've described and pretty soon your riding partners will be wondering how you make it look so easy.

A QUICK AND EASY CHECKUP

By Jim Langley

It's Friday night. The club century is tomorrow. You're carbo-loaded, super-hydrated, and your clothes are laid out. But is your bike ready?

Even new or just-repaired machines ought to be checked before every major event—preferably with enough time for a thorough test ride. It's the only way to catch the small problems that can lead to a mechanical breakdown, or worse, an accident.

This routine tune-up should take about an hour. Once you have the tools, it's manageable by the average home mechanic. Besides fixing any glitches, it will boost your confidence that you can handle anything that might happen on the big day. Keep in mind that this procedure works only on reasonably maintained bikes in good condition. If yours is suffering from years of neglect, it may need a complete overhaul (including repacking bearings).

Here's what you'll need to do the job right.

○ Allen wrenches (4-, 5-, and 6-millimeter)

○ Awl

○ Brake pads, four

○ Bucket

○ Chain lube

○ Combination wrench (10-millimeter)

○ Crank bolt wrench

○ Degreaser

- ◯ Detergent
- ◯ Headset wrenches
- ◯ Long screwdriver
- ◯ Pedal wrench
- ◯ Pump
- ◯ Rags
- ◯ Repair stand
- ◯ Spoke wrench
- ◯ Sponge
- ◯ Spray cleaner/polish
- ◯ Tires

1. Place the bike in a repair stand (outdoors, if possible). If it's only slightly dirty, apply a spray cleaner/polish made for bicycles to the frame and parts, then wipe with rags. For a filthy bike, remove both wheels and put a long screwdriver through the rear dropouts and chain. If the drivetrain is really grimy, spray the chain and derailleurs  with degreaser and let the bike sit for a few minutes. Fill the bucket with warm, soapy water. Wet an old sponge, hold it on the chain, and turn the crank to draw the chain through the sponge until the links sparkle (see photo). Clean the crankset and derailleurs as well. Then clean the frame and parts (including the wheels) with a fresh sponge. Rinse by dripping water from above. (Don't spray directly at the bike because this can force water into the bearings.) Dry the bike and parts with rags.

2. Stand in front of the bike, holding the fork in one hand and the down tube in the other. Push and pull on the fork to check for play in the headset. Rotate the fork slowly from side to side to feel for roughness. If it's loose or tight, adjust nut-style headsets by loosening the top nut with a headset wrench or large adjustable, then

slightly tighten or loosen the cone (underneath the top nut) with another. Next, tighten the top nut against the cone while you hold it in place (see photo). For threadless headsets loosen the stem binder bolts, then remove play or tightness by adjusting the allen screw atop the stem, and finish by securing the stem bolts. Now check the bottom bracket bearings. Stand beside the frame, hold the crankarms, and push and pull, feeling for play. Most modern bottom brackets are sealed and reliable. If yours is loose, have a shop remove the crankarms and adjust it.

3. Inspect the tires for sidewall cracks, tread cuts, and baldness. Replace tires, as needed. If you find anything embedded in the tread, pick it out with an awl (see photo). Also, check tire seating. There are molded lines on the base of the sidewalls that should sit just above the rim all the way around. If they dip below the rim edge or rise above it, the tire will roll poorly and possibly blow off. If you find these problems, de-

flate the tire and reinflate it, making sure that it seats correctly. Inflate both tires to the maximum pressure marked on the sidewall. Install the wheels on the bike, making sure that they are centered in the frame and the quick-releases are snug.

4. Starting at the valve stem, work your way around each wheel, wiggling the spokes to see if any are loose. After a few spokes, you'll get a feel for the correct tension. Keep in mind that the left-side spokes on the rear wheel are always looser than the others —just make sure that they are evenly tensioned compared with each other. If you find  loose spokes, tighten them by turning the nipple clockwise (when sighted from above) in half-turn increments. Then spin the wheels and sight trueness by looking at the gap between the rim and brake pad (see photo). True the wheel, if necessary. To move the rim to the left, loosen right-side nipples and tighten left-side nipples in the problem area. Do the reverse to move it right. Always turn nipples a half-turn at a time and check progress.

5. Though major components shouldn't loosen with normal use, it's wise to check them with the appropriate wrenches. Without forcing, try to tighten the crank bolts, pedals, chainring bolts (don't forget  those for the inner ring if you have a triple crankset), stem binder, handlebar binder, seat binder, seat bolt, brake and derailleur attaching nuts/bolts, and the rack and bottle cage screws. (Everything is turned clockwise to tighten except the left pedal, which is turned counterclockwise.) Also, remove and test your frame pump. If it doesn't inflate properly, try unscrewing the top, extracting the rod, and adding grease to the plunger (see photo). Check your patch kit. Does it have patches? Has the glue evaporated? If so, replace it. Finally, put a

drop of lube on the pivot points of clipless pedals, derailleurs, and brakes.

6. Lube shift cables where they pass under the bottom bracket. Lube the chain, then shift through the gears repeatedly to test derailleur adjustments. Because the rear derailleur's cable is longer and gets more use, it's more likely to go out of adjustment. Each click of the rear shift lever should cause the  chain to immediately jump to the next cog. If not, the cable has probably stretched slightly, or you may have mistakenly adjusted it too tightly. If the chain hesitates to go to a larger cog, the cable is slightly loose, or vice versa. Fix slow shifts to larger cogs by turning the adjustment barrel on the rear of the derailleur counterclockwise in half-turn increments (see photo). For slow shifts to smaller cogs, do the opposite.

7. Inspect the brake pads. If the grooves are worn away, replace the pads. Make sure that they strike the rim squarely. If not, loosen the nut with an allen wrench or 10-millimeter wrench and reposition them. Squeeze the brake levers to feel the action. The pads should strike the rim well before the levers approach the handlebar.  If not, tighten the brake by turning the barrels on the brake calipers. If it's one piece, turn it counterclockwise until the pads are ⅛ to ¼ inch away from the rim. If the barrel has two pieces, turn the large-diameter ring on the barrel clockwise to tighten the brake. (You may have to lift the barrel to get the

ring to turn.) If the pads don't release equally, center the brake with the small screw above (for Shimanos, see photo) or allen on the side (for Campagnolos) of the brake arm. On old-style brakes slightly loosen the attaching nut behind the brake, center the caliper, then tighten the nut. Or, look for flats on the pivot bolt (next to the frame) that allow centering with a thin wrench.

8. Test-ride the bike. Shift and brake repeatedly, then fine-tune adjustments, if necessary. If the brakes squeak, determine which one is making the noise. Adjust the pads on that brake by toeing them slightly. (Make each pad's leading edge strike the rim slightly before the trailing edge.) Many pads, such as those from Campagnolo, have washers that permit toeing  the pad after loosening the nut. If the pads don't include toeing hardware, it's possible to adjust them by bending the brake arm (see photo) with an adjustable wrench. (Adjust the jaws to just slide over the arm.) But be careful, or you might break the brake.

TWO

Essential Skills

Breathe Better to Ride Better

LUNG POWER

By Davis Phinney

When I asked one of my cycling friends if he thought much about his breathing, he replied, "No, but I'm a firm believer in it."

Breathing is strongly emphasized and controlled in activities such as swimming, singing, and yoga, but it's rarely given a second thought by cyclists. By working on your breathing technique, however, you can significantly improve your riding.

Most riders breathe primarily through their mouths and use only a small percentage of their lungs. Because they don't concentrate on breathing, they don't learn to maximize lung capacity. I learned this from one of my mentors, Polish world road champion Stan Szozda. He spent considerable time developing his lungs. According to him the secret to success is breathing, and the way to improve it is through regular training. Each day, he would inhale to his maximum and hold it, stretching his lungs to capacity. He carried this over to swimming, trying to go as far as possible underwater (hypoxic training). He believed that lungs lose flexibility and capacity without training, just as muscles do. Whenever Szozda wound up his road sprint, you could hear him coming by the sound of his intense exhalations. He was a master at hilltop finishes and long sprints because of his ability to control his breathing. Here are four ways to improve yours.

Stretch your diaphragm. Anyone who grew up watching the old *Superman* TV series got the wrong idea. I figured that by lifting my shoulders and sticking out my chest I could blow down buildings. I was wrong. The key is the stomach. By pushing it in and out, not up and down, you are best able to access your full lung capacity because you are using your diaphragm muscle.

Adopt a new rhythm. To gain control of your breathing, concentrate on a specific pattern of inhaling and exhaling, then coordinate it with your pedal stroke. This idea has been expounded by numerous people, most notably Ian Jackson in his book *Breath Play*. Skip Hamilton, a cycling coach and member of *Bicycling* magazine's record-breaking team in the 1996 Race Across America, has worked with Jackson and simplified the approach.

Hamilton teaches breathing in varied rhythms because most riders tend to fall into one set pattern while riding, especially on hard climbs. For instance, they always exhale with the same-side downstroke, and they often breathe in for half a stroke and out for half a stroke. For most people this means breathing out as they push down with the right leg.

To change the pattern, exhale longer every few breaths. You'll automatically change your rhythm. Hamilton calls this switch-side breathing. You will be breathing out on both the left- and the right-side downstroke over the course of a ride. Cyclists who try this simple technique report that it gives them a feeling of fresher legs—almost like having an extra gear.

Switch-side breathing is only a starting point, though. I have tried many variations. For instance, by counting pedal strokes, I extend the length of each breath. Eventually, you'll become aware of balancing your breathing and pedaling. Play with any number of patterns and breathing techniques, such as the following:

❍ Even breathing. Try a rhythm where you take long, even breaths and begin exhaling at the top of a stroke. Alternate legs each time. By tying your breath to the pedal stroke, you are less likely to exhale incompletely and start gasping. Use a consistent gear and effort. Try counting, "1, 2, 3, in; 4, 5, 6, out."

❍ Quick in, long out. U.S. cyclist Alexi Grewal, the 1984 Olympic road champion, used to work on exhaling as slowly as possible—like a weight lifter timing the push phase with a breath. Because cycling is pretty much a continuous push phase, he would inhale deeply and quickly (1-2 count) then slowly exhale (3-4-5 count), like air leaking from a balloon.

Breathe through your nose. In a book called *Body, Mind, and Sport*, author John Douillard advocates nasal breathing exclusively during exercise as a way to a Zen-like experience. I have yet to meet anyone who has achieved enlightenment by using this technique, but athletes who have tried it report that it's a good tool for controlling effort. The amount of air that you can inhale through your nose is limited, so it acts like a natural governor on your pace. Your performance capacity rises because when you use both your nose and mouth, efficiency improves.

Legend has it that Apache warriors used to prepare for the rigors of the desert by taking long runs with their mouths full of water. The reasoning was sound. Focusing on holding in the water without swallowing taught mental discipline. Breathing through the nose taught moderation of intensity in order to endure the distance. Not breathing heavily through the mouth slowed dehydration from vapor loss. Wisdom of the ancients. One caution, though: It's easy to overdo nasal breathing. You don't want to hyperventilate.

Open your nostrils. Anyone who watches professional sports is bound to notice tape on some athletes' noses. This product is making its way into the cycling world, too. The principle is simple: The device is actually a spring that pulls the sides of the nose to expand nasal passages. How much this actually adds to performance is uncertain. During efforts at more than 80 percent of maximum, almost all of a rider's breathing takes place through the mouth. Even so, anything that can help air get into the body is worth considering.

What will mastering these techniques do for your cycling? Imagine ascending a tough hill. As you approach the climb, you focus on breathing. Taking even, measured breaths, your body stays relaxed. As the hill steepens, you back off slightly, adjusting your output to match the effort needed. Instead of tensing you are fluid—even though the effort gets progressively more difficult. Because you are closely monitoring your breathing, you are also keenly aware of your heart rate. In this way the hill seems to pass harmlessly under your wheels. You're already rolling toward the next one as you actively recover.

Remember, use these breathing techniques as tools, but don't let them dominate your rides.

Slow Down without Wasting Speed

BRAKING AWAY

By Davis Phinney

Braking is one of those skills you learn early in your cycling career. My five-year-old son found this out the hard way as we were ripping down the hill to school, a tad late for kindergarten. Taylor drifted toward a parked car. I could see him start to correct his line and simultaneously hit the brake. Oops! Coaster brakes can be pretty unforgiving, and this time he locked the rear wheel, causing the bike to move sideways. Instead of steering past the car, he smacked right into the side of it and fell in a heap.

Anyone who has spent much time on a road bike is familiar with my son's experience. When confronted with an unexpected obstacle, you need to respond in a calculated way—or you might end up in a heap, too.

A LIGHT TOUCH

Although you'll ride most often with your hands on the brake hoods, maximum control on descents comes in the handlebar drops. For proof, look at pictures of the pros. They put their hands in the drops with one finger extended to each brake lever. This is known as feathering the brakes. More fingers around the handlebar means a better grip, and modern brakes work effectively with the strength of just one finger. I have seen numerous accidents caused by a rider pulling the lever with a full fist. When you grab quickly with too much force (or, like my son, by mashing down on the pedal), the likely results are skidding and loss of control. Try using just one or two fingers—even for panic stops. If you feel that your hands are too weak for this, try squeezing a tennis ball regularly to strengthen them.

Equipment setup is important, too. Start by making sure that the levers fit your hands. Short-reach levers are available for riders with small hands. Women should consider this option rather than struggling with the full-size levers that most bikes come with.

Be sure that the levers pull freely. Keep the brake cables and pivot points lubed. The cable housing should run relatively straight (no kinks). Also, make sure that the pads strike the rim at the same time. If your brakes are out of alignment, they'll pull the wheel over, causing a subtle adverse affect on your steering.

HANDLING TURNS

The main reason to brake is usually for an upcoming corner.

When you enter a corner, you should have already slowed so that you don't have to apply the brakes while turning. Approach the corner and stay off the brakes until just before entering, which helps you maintain speed. I prefer this to slowing gradually and endlessly riding the brakes between turns. Apply both brakes evenly as you come in, and establish your line. By the apex you should be off the brakes completely and in control so that you can carry speed out of the turn. Also, make sure to keep your weight back. Braking tends to push you forward, loading the front wheel and making maneuvering more difficult.

I don't prefer one brake over the other, but I do use my dominant (left) hand to control my rear brake. This is because I can control a rear-brake skid much more easily than a front one.

Many riders mistakenly think that the front brake should never be used alone, but a light touch will go a long way toward keeping you in control. Too much front brake can wash the bike out from under you, though, in even faintly slick conditions, and a heavy hand on the front brake can also make the bike more difficult to steer. Don't be afraid to use it, but do so deftly.

One final rule: The harder you brake while turning, the more upright your bike wants to be. And the more upright it is, the less it wants to turn. This has important implications when you enter a turn with too much speed and attempt to save yourself.

I remember racing on a high ridge road in northern California. I was leading the pack as we started to drop into a valley. Using the lead motorcycle as a gauge, I let it fly. As we blasted into one of the first corners, I realized too late that it was very tight. Pushing the bike over as far as I dared, I was tempted to grab the brakes as hard as possible. Instead, I feathered them. The two guys behind me locked them up hard.

PHINNEY'S RULES FOR BRAKING

○ Feather the brakes. Use just one or two fingers.

○ Brake before a turn. Applying the brakes while turning makes your bike more upright and harder to turn.

○ Keep your weight back. Braking loads the front wheel, making maneuvering difficult.

○ Use the front brake lightly. Too much force makes it tougher to steer.

○ Sometimes it's safer *not* to brake. You can handle sharper, faster turns.

Predictably, their bikes straightened up, and they went straight off the road (along with the motorcycle).

The amazing thing was that as I hung on, pushing my line right to the edge of the road, another guy actually dove inside me. As the jersey flashed by, I saw it was none other than off-road champion John Tomac, one of the best bike handlers on the planet. Figures. Later, he told me that I shouldn't brake so much.

QUICK AND SAFE CORNERING

By Davis Phinney

Riding around a corner should be easy. Picture a rivulet of water as it snakes its way down the gutter. Following the most natural line, the fluid flows and banks as it is pulled by gravity along the route that best maintains momentum. What could be more natural?

Until the moment when my bike and I hit the guardrail and sailed into a vineyard in the south of France, I thought that I knew how to flow. After all, my reputation and career were based on my ability to fly through the final turn of a criterium and be the first guy across the finish line. But as I lay in the brambles—scuffed, scratched, half-senseless—one thing rang clear: I had taken cornering skills for granted. When faced with an unthinkably steep, twisting Pyrenees descent, my technique just didn't cut it.

Since that day, I have schooled myself on the basics of cornering, constantly evaluating how a bike turns and how it might turn better. Even now, several years after my pro road racing career ended, every ride involves some form of turning practice. We also teach these skills at our Carpenter/Phinney Bike Camps, where everyone spends an afternoon riding around cones in a parking lot. By riding in the same environment, you can practice the techniques I'll discuss, learning to believe in yourself and your bike. Always use a safe place away from traffic. And don't practice in the close company of other riders, where a mistake can cause a crash.

I like to break cornering into three styles, based on the correlation of your body to the bike and the differing angles of lean of both bike and body. If you learn the mechanics of these styles, I guarantee your riding will be safer and more fun, regardless of your type of cycling.

Upright steering. The more upright the bike, the less chance there is that it will slide out from under you. Taking advantage of this maxim, one school of thought recommends that you corner with your bike as upright as possible, simply by turning the handlebar like a steering wheel.

This works in certain conditions, such as when the pavement is slippery from moisture, oil, or gravel. It's prudent to keep the bike vertical and steer it over the slick stuff at a slower (and thereby safer) speed. This keeps sideways force to a minimum and directs traction downward. The problem is that when a bike is upright it has a hard time turning at speeds above 15 miles per hour. To corner quickly with this technique, you have to lean your upper body toward the inside of the turn. So, in most instances I've found this to be the least efficient method of turning. It makes you top-heavy, and modifying your line is virtually impossible once you have committed.

Inclination. At faster speeds—and especially through shallower turns—the bike will make a nice, safe, wide arc if you just lean it over. In skiing this is called inclination. This is probably the most common way of cornering. Nothing fancy, it's just a matter of leaning body and bike together and following the natural line. You really don't need to do anything but push through ("weight") your outside pedal (which should be at the 6 o'clock position), and lean with the bike as much as needed to accomplish the turn.

The only way to predict how much lean is required at certain speeds through different turns is to play with it. In unfamiliar territory I like to use this turning style only through consistent, arcing turns where I can see the exit clearly. You need faith that your tires won't slide out. Good tires won't unless really pushed. As one who has tested the limits, I can vouch for it. I've also found that this method works well on wet asphalt, if it isn't oily.

Countersteering. Now let's get fancy and talk about countersteering, the most valuable cornering principle in my opinion. It's the quickest way to get the bike through a turn, yet it still allows you to make corrections while leaning.

To understand countersteering, ride down a straight road or parking lot with no traffic, get into the drops, and as the speed builds see what happens when you quickly press down with your left hand. The bike heels left, then veers right. Initially, this simple principle is all there is to it. At speed a bike wants to turn when angled, and the easiest way to angle it is to lever the front wheel over by pushing the handlebar away from the direction you want to turn.

No way, you say? Try it. Push the bar away from the turn. Your bike will nod in the direction you push, then quickly react by diving toward the opposite side, which means into the turn. As you spend more time with countersteering, work on the riding position that helps it happen. Keep your hands in the drops. Weight the outside pedal. Let your inside knee point into the turn. Straighten your inside arm as you push that side of the handlebar down—not with the quick punch that initiated the countersteer but with continual pressure.

For good form while countersteering, point the inside knee into the turn and straighten the inside arm, pushing the handlebar down to angle the bike away from the body.

Should you come upon something unexpected while turning, the beauty of countersteering will really shine. You can change your line instantly by either putting more pressure on the inside of the handlebar (which tightens your turn radius), or pulling the bike upright underneath you (which broadens the radius). Just remember that bringing the bike upright significantly decreases your ability to get around the turn. So once you're past the obstacle, you'll need to push the inside bar down and continue turning.

Stay relaxed. Keeping loose on the bike allows you to move around and subtly influence its line through the turn. As the bike banks, your body naturally centers itself in juxtaposition to the angle of the bike. (In skiing this technique is called angulation. It is the process of staying centered over the main part of your mass while making turns.)

Descending and braking tend to push your body forward, which loads the front wheel. Counteract this by pushing back on the saddle and flattening your upper body along the length of the bike to get better weight distribution.

THE PAYOFF

In 1990, I was suffering through a bad day in the Tour de France. On the stage to Luz Ardiden and with two major climbs to go, I struggled over the summit with teammate Sean Yates. We were facing a 10-kilometer descent before the steep Col du Tourmalet.

Without speaking we fired down the treacherous descent as if shot from a gun. Focusing only on the road before me, I hurtled into the rough turns, passing other stragglers as if they were glued to the pavement. It was one of the most exhilarating rides of my life because when crunch time came, I was ready. I had absolute faith that no matter what lay around the next bend, I'd have the skill and confidence to handle it.

Work on these cornering techniques and you can have this confidence, too.

ATTACKING HILLS

By Davis Phinney

During the early years of America's premier stage race, the Tour DuPont, we raced up one of the nastiest climbs in the Northeast. We called it the Devil's Kitchen, a 2-mile stretch of goat path with 12- to 14-percent grades. I started the hill at the front (like a good sprinter should) and witnessed an amazing climbing display. We thought that we had perfectly positioned our team leader, Andy Hampsten, so he could control the pace of the leaders, but we weren't prepared for the abilities of a lean Dutch rider, Gert-Jan Theunisse.

Who says that you have to come from the mountains to ride them well? Theunisse got off the saddle like he was casually getting up from the couch during a TV commercial break, then rode away from every-one. As I struggled mightily in my 39 × 23-tooth (39 × 23T) low gear, he pushed a 42 × 20T. Like a robot, he held his body still while turning that impossibly big gear and dropped Hampsten like a discarded water bottle. As rider after rider worked his way past my lumbering group of sprinters, I watched the fast-disappearing Dutchman give us a climb-ing primer.

Handling hills so steep that they threaten to rob you of momentum requires both technical fine-tuning and strength-building. These are the keys to progressing beyond survival-mode climbing. Here's the scoop on conquering the steeps.

BE A STAND-UP RIDER

When the gradient steepens, you will almost always be off the saddle to retain momentum. Unlike mountain biking, where you must sit down to maintain traction and your gearing is extremely low, road riding allows you to stand and get your weight over each pedal. Standing also means that you can access support muscles (arms and shoulders) that pull on the bar. Some riders can stay in the saddle and still get power from their torsos. It's a matter of individual style and strength. I spend much of the time out of the saddle because I can't keep my speed up when I sit down. Also, my lowest gear is a relatively high 39 × 23T, reflecting my racing heritage. To an old road dog like me, lower means slower.

Use long, gentle hills to practice moving from a seated to standing position. Your seated position should be with hands on the bar top near the stem. Pull lightly, with your shoulders and hips square. Keep your upper body relaxed to reduce energy cost and maximize lung capacity.

Before standing, switch your grip to the brake-lever hoods. Rise and bring your hips forward, straightening and lengthening your lower back and opening your chest. The saddle's nose should just brush the back of your legs. Don't pull with your arms too much on easy hills because it taxes your muscles with little return in speed. Let your weight help as you smoothly pull your body over one pedal, then over the other. Pull up on the right hood as you push down with your right foot, alternating right arm/right foot, left arm/left foot. The bike will rock subtly beneath you, establishing a rhythmic powering of the pedals.

Get off the saddle as much as necessary to climb longer hills comfortably. You can't stay out of the saddle forever (although I've seen some Colombians, fabled climbers, who seemingly could). For most riders standing is more fatiguing because it uses extra upper-body muscle, so keep it fairly short. Many riders alternate periods of sitting and standing on each climb. See what works for you.

STEEPER CHALLENGES

When you feel comfortable on shallow grades, head for steeper hills. I define "steep" as grades greater than 10 percent, but this differs substantially among riders, depending on fitness, gearing, and body weight. On steep grades come off the saddle and hold your bike as vertical as possible, with minimal sway. It's critical to keep your shoulders squared and facing forward. Don't drop them and create a snaking motion that wastes forward progress. In order to maintain momentum on a steep grade, you need to be rock-solid off the saddle. Many riders don't control their body and bike motion, making climbing a struggle. Work on being quiet and efficient.

If the grade threatens to rob your momentum completely and you are nearly at a standstill, try pulling back with both hands in unison on each downstroke. It lets you put maximum force into the pedals to keep the bike moving. Continue until the grade lessens and you can return to a normal climbing technique.

It's hard to relax during a climb, but remember that keeping your muscles constantly flexed will quickly wear you down. Climbing isn't sprinting—it's a measured effort. Use only the strength necessary to keep your momentum, no more. Gradually, you'll learn to maintain a controlled style while staying relaxed and breathing evenly. Truly steep grades, though, are tough no matter what you do.

THE SIZE ISSUE

What about the nonclimber's lament: "I'm too big to climb well!" Sure, how much you weigh definitely affects how much gravity abuses you. Light riders climb easier, especially on steep hills. Still, easier does not necessarily mean better or faster. Big riders with good fitness who make evenly paced efforts and use all available muscle resources can more than hold their own. Don't neglect building upper-body strength because you're afraid it will make you too heavy to climb well. I stopped worrying about carrying extra muscle in my arms when I found that as my upper body got stronger (from off-season Nordic skiing), my climbing got better.

Your strength-to-weight ratio is the key. The more you weigh, the more you need to build torso strength. Big riders pull much harder on the brake hoods because of their greater push on the pedals. Keeping your arms and stomach strong will enhance climbing. I recommend doing curls (forward and reverse) with light dumbbells. Crunches work the gut muscles that produce a direct transmission of power from the arms to the legs. Abdominal strength also reduces strain on your lower back.

Use all of these tips and you won't be cooked in your local Devil's Kitchen.

GOING DOWN

By Ed Pavelka

The hardship of a climb is usually followed by the joy of a descent. On a recreational ride you have two basic choices: coast and recover, or push for greater thrills. Either way, risk increases along with your speed, so it pays to practice the principles of expert descending.

First, don't end the climb too soon. Many riders ease up when they reach the crest of a hill. This is a natural response—muscles are tired and breathing is labored. But lots of momentum can be lost in the transition from climbing to descending. Keep pedaling strongly over the top until gravity takes hold and you're able to start shifting to higher gears. When you're moving well, you can soft-pedal to let your muscles recover for a moment. By having this bit of discipline on each hill, you'll be significantly faster on hilly terrain.

On an unfamiliar descent, especially one with curves, it pays to be cautious. Any number of hazards may be around the next bend: gravel, sand, driveways, animals, broken pavement, a plank bridge, maybe even a stop sign at a busy intersection. A sudden hairpin turn may appear, too, catching you going too fast. Temper your speed by feathering the brakes with a finger on each lever. Keep your weight back, but sit up to let more air catch your chest. As for any corner, apply the brakes before entering, not after you're already leaning in.

Sometimes you'll be with a rider who knows the descent. Assuming that you are of fairly equal ability, let him take the lead. Simply trace his line down the hill. Hang back several lengths so that, if a mistake is made, you'll have time to adjust and not suffer the same fate. There's no benefit to following tight on a wheel while descending.

Always look well ahead to see what's coming. Keep your line fluid

Descending with hands on the brake hoods lets you sit up to see better and breathe easier.

by thinking about the turn beyond the one you're approaching. Traffic permitting, use the entire lane to make turns shallower, which means less risk of the bike sliding out. For example, be at the center line when approaching a right turn. Dive through at the apex and emerge either along the road edge or center line, depending on whether the next turn is left or right, respectively.

Here are some other tips and techniques to ensure that your descents are fun and safe.

❍ It's not necessary to keep a low, streamlined position while descending. By sitting up with your hands on the brake hoods, you can see better and breathe easier to recover from the climb. Most riders won't find it difficult to brake effectively from the top of the levers.

❍ Wear sunglasses to protect your eyes from injury by bugs and other airborne objects. Shades will also stop cold air that could make your eyes water uncontrollably. If you suddenly can't see on a fast, curvy descent, it could get nasty.

❍ Descend in a high gear, but not necessarily the highest. You may need to pedal through a flatter section or two on the way down. Even when rolling too fast to pedal, revolve your legs slowly to prevent muscles from tightening and cramping.

❍ If hard braking is necessary, apply both brakes simultaneously. The front has more power because your weight is moving forward, but using it without the rear can make the bike hard to control. Using the rear brake alone will almost surely cause the wheel to lock up and skid.

❍ When coasting, keep the crankarms horizontal. This lets your feet help your arms and butt support your body weight and absorb road shock. As you enter each turn, place the outside pedal down and press hard on it.

❍ Try the countersteering technique discussed in chapter 7. Extend your torso to the outside of the turn while pushing the handlebar down to the inside. This accentuates the turning effect while actually decreasing the chance of skidding.

❍ Above all, stay relaxed. Once these techniques are ingrained, your bike should feel as if it's flowing down the hill. It's hard to beat the excitement of fast, yet safe, descending. Soon, you will be searching for climbs because of the fun that's on the other side.

SPRINT LIKE A CHAMPION

By Davis Phinney

A big field sprint is the most exciting part of cycling. Spoken like a true sprinter, huh? My two Tour de France stage wins and dozens of other sprint victories provided plenty of heart-stoppers and earned me the moniker Cash Register. But one stands out.

In the 1991 Tour DuPont, the 100-mile first stage ended on a long hill in Wilmington, Delaware. Coming into the finish, I jumped on the train of Phil Anderson's teammates, who were setting him up for the win. As the lone member of a different team, I stuck out like a frozen link in a chain.

Sean Yates ripped down the back straight, Ron Kiefel cranked through the corners, and Steve Bauer took over when we made the turn to the finish line. I sat poised in Bauer's draft, with Anderson on my wheel. Perfect position, I thought—until Bauer looked back, saw me, and shut down, pulling off to the side. It was now or never for me. I was in a 53 × 15-tooth (53 × 15T) gear with 350 uphill yards to go. I jumped hard, wound up the 15T quickly, hit the shift, and accelerated in the 14T. Another 100 yards, and no one had passed. Pop! I dropped it into the 13T. With 50 yards to go, the hill flattened and the last shift put me into the 12T. I was close to blacking out from the anaerobic effort, but my arms flew up in victory on the line. The sprint lasted well over 30 seconds, off the saddle the whole way, with three shifts. Anderson was unable to make up an inch.

But why hone your sprint if you aren't a competitive rider? What good is speed if your cycling goal is fitness and fun?

First, sprinting is play—a burst of energy and speed, like when a child runs from friends in a game of tag. It's fun to sprint for town signs with your training buddies. It enlivens rides and improves your fitness. In emergencies it's more intense, like a primal burst of competitive rage, an explosion. How about that unseen dog bolting at you? Or the car that doesn't quite make the yellow light and barrels through the intersection? A quick burst of speed can save your life. And for many riders, cycling is a numbers game. We like to test our limits. How fast can you go? Not downhill, but under your own power on a flat road with no wind.

Here are some basic sprinting techniques to help you ring up some "victories" of your own.

○ To set up for a sprint, choose a slightly larger gear than the one you can roll along in comfortably. Grasp the handlebar firmly, deep in the drops.

○ Start your sprint by coming off the saddle as your pedal goes past the 12 o'clock position. It doesn't matter which foot you start with. If you kick with your right foot, you'll probably feel more natural using that one.

○ Commit everything to the effort. Pull strongly with the arm that's on the same side as the pushing foot, counteracting your leg's downward force. But keep both arms fairly rigid so that the bike stays upright under you.

○ At first, keep your weight back so that the rear wheel gets good traction during the early, high-torque phase. Hold your body square to the bike. Let your hips and shoulders work in unison just like when you're climbing out of the saddle.

○ As you pick up speed, relax. Alternately pull and release the bar in sync with your downstrokes. Slowly rotate forward, keeping your body fairly low for better aerodynamics. Don't let your legs straighten completely at the bottom of each stroke. You want constant, fluid power going to the pedals. Keep your head as low as you can while still seeing where you're going.

SHIFTING WHILE SPRINTING

Most sprints are initiated out of the saddle. But once you get rolling, you have a choice. Classically, track sprinters on fixed gears sit down and spin to the line. I was a power road rider, so I pushed a big gear

(53 × 12T) and stayed out of the saddle the whole way. This let me use my arms throughout the effort.

In the old days, with down-tube-mounted shifters, sprinting was a gamble. You picked one gear for the whole sprint, from the jump to the finish, and hoped that you made the right choice. An excessively low gear meant spinning out, while a high gear cost energy to get going. To shift you had to sit down, reach for the gear lever, then stand again. It was awkward and sure to disrupt your momentum.

Now, combined brake/shift lever systems (Shimano STI and Campagnolo Ergopower) have revolutionized sprinting. You can jump into a lower (easier) gear, build speed quickly, then shift by tapping the appropriate lever, all at full throttle out of the saddle. I like STI, which shifts only one cog at a time so there's almost no risk of a misshift in the heat of a sprint. By tapping the upshift lever with my index finger, my revolutions-per-minute and effort stay constant.

SPEED TRAINING

I prefer to train alone for sprinting. You don't need a training partner to experience the joy of blasting down the road full tilt while improving your fitness. Try these four solo sprint workouts.

Spin sprints. Use gravity to improve your seated-sprinting form. Spin downhill at 120 to 150 revolutions per minute, choosing a gear that enables you to keep tension on the chain for 10 seconds or so. Repeat three to eight times. Concentrate on staying relaxed and pedaling in circles.

If you bounce wildly on the saddle, use a slightly bigger gear. Low-gear accelerations are the best way to improve your pedal stroke and build leg speed.

Short sprints. Pick a road sign or telephone pole about 100 yards away. Jump out of the saddle in a lower gear (say, 42 × 16T). After this initial burst, you can opt to sit or remain standing, depending on your style. Try five to 10 reps with full recovery in between. This sprint builds explosive power and leg speed. It's also good practice for getting away from dogs.

Progressive shifting. If you have brake/shift levers, roll easily on a flat road, then jump strongly. Shift every 50 to 100 yards as you begin to spin out the gear. Aim for two to three shifts without losing speed. For instance, jump in a 53 × 16T, then go to 15T, 14T, 13T. This should take about 30 seconds. Do it two to four times during a workout to build sprint endurance as well as shifting technique.

Hill sprints. Find a gradual hill 200 to 400 yards long. Roll up halfway, then shift into the big chainring (say, 53 × 17T) and sprint over the top. Try two to five reps with complete recovery between efforts. It's essential to maintain good form. This sprint will do wonders for your strength. Former pro Ron Kiefel, one of the best hilltop finishers in the world, used this workout religiously. You need a strong fitness base to do it right.

Add these workouts to your solo rides. Then, as you gain confidence, find a partner or a group and play with competition. You'll rediscover that momentary burst of energy you had as a child when the only thing that mattered was escaping being "it."

GROUP RIDING

By Geoff Drake

Road cycling, for all its virtues, is almost Victorian in its codes of dress and behavior. There is, for example, the sin of unmatched clothing, the sin of the tipped-back helmet, the sin of hairy legs, and, of course, the sin of bad group-riding etiquette.

Experienced cyclists will tell you, though, that parts of this code make sense, particularly when it comes to etiquette. Smooth, predictable riding when you're in a group isn't just a matter of style, it's survival. Here are the rules of riding steadily.

Leading. Ever notice how easy some cyclists are to ride behind? Their path on the road seems drawn by a draftsman's tools, and their tempo has the steadiness of an electric motor. In short when you're on the wheel of one of these cyclists, life is good.

How does one become such a paragon of predictability? The first step is to understand that you're responsible for the rider(s) behind you. You hold the joystick. This means that you can speed them up, slow them down—or make them crash.

Start by visualizing a string tied between your saddle and the following rider's handlebar. Imagine that sudden accelerations will break this string (leaving your pal behind) and quick stops will make it slacken (causing him to overlap your wheel and lunch on tarmac). Your job is to keep the string taut. This doesn't necessarily mean maintaining the same speed. Instead, concentrate on exerting the same pedal pressure. This means that slowing slightly for hills is okay.

Remember, too, that just touching your brakes while riding at the front will set off general alarms to the rear. Feather the front brake only and continue pedaling against it. This moderates speed without disturbing trailing riders. If you must brake hard, such as for a dog, announce "Stopping!" or "Slowing!" Another way to control speed without braking is to simply sit up and let the wind slow you. In any case continue pedaling.

Holding a line. It's likely that, despite a thousand cautions, the person behind is going to overlap your wheel. If you swerve while this is happening and touch wheels, that person is going down. Period. What's more, despite the error, he will think twice about cycling with you again.

To avoid this, ride as if you're on rails. On occasion this means going over a bump that you would otherwise swerve to avoid. The same theory applies to bunnyhopping obstacles. Reserve this move for solo entertainment and times when you have plenty of airspace.

Larger obstacles, such as parked cars, and road debris merit verbal and hand warnings. As leader it is your job to scan the road for this flotsam and call it out, "Move left!" or "Glass!"

When cornering, follow the expected line. This means starting wide, gradually cutting to the apex, then swinging wide again. Save your early- or late-apex turns and other fancy stuff for riding alone.

Using hand signals. I rarely use hand signals when riding alone. I believe lane position and looking behind says enough, but signaling a turn is never a bad idea in traffic—or in a group. Let others know your intention by sticking your arm directly out toward whichever way you're turning. (This is much more effective than holding up your left hand to indicate a right turn.) If the group is large, go a step further and yell, "Left turn!" or whatever the case may be. Others should help telegraph it to the back of the bunch.

Climbing. Perhaps the most common new-rider *faux pas* is "drop kicking" the person behind when standing to climb. This occurs because cadence naturally decreases as you rise from the saddle, causing your bike to slow down. The rider behind then hits your rear wheel, with the inevitable result. Usually the situation is exacerbated by both parties being in oxygen debt and not being in full possession of their faculties.

To avoid this, shift to the next higher gear before standing to compensate for the slower cadence and maintain pressure on the pedals so that your bike doesn't move "backward" relative to the rider behind.

This sit/stand transition takes practice but soon becomes automatic. Concentrate on eliminating any freewheeling as you stand. You should always feel resistance through the pedals.

The same thing applies when you sit again. Downshift and concentrate on maintaining pedal pressure to avoid any abrupt change in speed.

Following. Never overlap wheels. Instead, stay at least 6 inches behind a smooth, reliable rider, and much farther back if you don't know the person. One frequent cause of running up on someone is "freewheel fixation"—becoming mesmerized while staring at the wheel in front (made worse, again, by oxygen debt). Instead, look "through" the lead rider, scanning for trouble. Remember this rule: Look at nothing but see everything.

One caveat: It's true that experienced cyclists routinely overlap wheels to gain shelter in a crosswind. (This type of paceline is called an echelon.) But such a combination of skill and cooperation is rare. Don't trust riders you don't know.

Handling traffic. When you're following other riders, it's common to announce an overtaking vehicle, particularly if one of your pals is out in the road too far. A quick, "Car back!" will let those ahead know that it's wise to tuck in so the traffic can pass.

When leading, some riders like to announce, "Clear!" when they see an intersection is free of traffic, thus allowing the rest of the group to sail through unimpeded. Be careful with this. Sometimes it's better to let others survey the intersection for themselves. Then they won't blame you for any close calls.

Looking behind. If you're in a double paceline or riding beside someone in a large group, and you want to look back (such as for a rider who has fallen behind), first rest your hand on your neighbor's shoulder. This provides a stable reference point and will keep you moving straight ahead. We all tend to swerve a little when we look behind, and in a pack that can spell trouble.

Pulling through. In the next chapter the intricacies of paceline formations are covered. But one important point is worth emphasizing here. In any situation where you're sharing the work by alternating the front position, don't surge. Check your cyclecomputer before you get to the front and maintain the same speed as you pull through. Once you've done your time, look over your shoulder for traffic (which also serves as a signal to other riders), pull off without accelerating, and slow a bit so that you drift to the back. Keep pedaling and swing out only as far as necessary to clear the group (about a handlebar width). At the back of the pack is the least disruptive time to eat or take a swig from your bottle.

Practice these techniques, and you will be easy to recognize on the road: You will be the one with legions of cyclists pedaling happily behind you.

Ensuring That You Pull Your Weight

PACELINE RIDING

By Davis Phinney

ew types of cycling are as exhilarating—or potentially as frighten-
ing—as paceline riding. In the 1989 Tour of Italy team time trial,
nine of us were flying along at close to 35 miles per hour, wheels no
more than 4 inches apart. We knew that we were among the top five
teams overall. Sean Yates, the great English rider, was applying pressure
at the front. Suddenly, a black cat darted across the road, straight into
Yates's front wheel. Bob Roll, the next rider in line, took a hard right
to miss him. This caused six guys to go sprawling across the road.
Amazingly, no one was seriously injured. But we did donate considerable skin to the Italian tarmac.

The black cat hissed and ran off, unscathed.

Despite occasional mishaps, sharing the pace allows you to ride
faster and with less effort. The keys are working together, building
trust, and paying attention. At the elite level, pacelines (or echelons)
become art forms, moving like a squadron of fighter pilots in a constantly flowing rhythm. But recreational riders can benefit, too. In a
century, riding in a group will allow you to finish faster and fresher.
Busting a headwind isn't much fun alone, but with a few others to
help, the miles pass quickly.

An added bonus: You get to the rest stops sooner, guaranteeing the
best pastry selection.

THE FUNDAMENTALS

Why do many riders choose to go it alone? Club rides can turn into
macho free-for-alls, where the novice is quickly sent off the back. Ide-

Sharing the effort is critical to maintaining a smooth paceline.

ally, a group should contain both rookies and experienced riders who don't feel compelled to prove themselves on every ride.

Pacelines are either single or double. In a single paceline everyone lines up behind the first rider, who maintains a constant speed. The rotation occurs when the front rider pulls off to the side and drifts to the back of the line. The next rider then sets the pace. Riders stay on the front from a few seconds to several minutes. This type of paceline has the advantage of requiring minimal road space.

A double echelon, also known as a rotating paceline, contains two lines of riders side by side, continuously in motion. (An echelon, therefore, requires a wide shoulder or a low-traffic road.) One line goes slightly faster than the other. Let's say that you're the lead rider in the faster line. You should cross over to the slow line after passing the front wheel of the rider beside you. Then you drift back with the others in the slow line. When the final position is reached (back of the line), you slide onto the back wheel of the last rider in the fast line. What this formation looks like is a constantly rotating elliptical chain.

If you're confused, gather several friends and walk through the fundamentals in your living room. Try a single echelon first. Lead for 10 seconds, then pull off either to the right or left and slide to the back of the line. Stay close enough to bump elbows, then move in behind the last person. Now try the double paceline. Form two lines, side by side. March up the faster line, pull over to the front of the slower line, then drop back with it. Practice both clockwise and counterclockwise rotations.

Next, adjust to crosswinds. Wind direction determines which way to pull off—you always move into a crosswind. This way the advancing line, which is already working harder, gets some protection from the wind. In strong crosswinds riders become offset like geese on the wing. They also overlap wheels, which means a mistake can take down the whole bunch. The width of this type of paceline also requires a completely traffic-free road.

REFINING YOUR SKILLS

By walking through the basics, you have already started to form some trust with your group. But before you try these skills on the road, here are 10 tips for becoming a master of the echelon.

○ Put weaker riders behind stronger ones.

○ A paceline is a team. It's only as strong as its weakest member, so help that person.

○ Start by riding slowly in low gears.

○ Get used to following closely to get the benefit of the draft. Top riders feel comfortable riding within inches of the wheel in front. In a rotating paceline stay just as close side to side.

○ Ride smoothly and predictably. Never accelerate or brake quickly. If you are running up on the wheel in front, slow down (without braking) by moving into the wind slightly.

○ Maintain a constant speed when you get to the front by glancing at your cyclecomputer. (The tendency is to accelerate.)

○ If the rider at the front charges off, let that person go and hold your speed. If you're in a double echelon, move over and fill the hole just created.

○ If you tire, sit out as many turns as necessary by staying at the back. Let riders coming back know that you are resting, and give them space to move in ahead of you.

○ As the speed increases, gaps may develop because riders can't hold the wheel ahead, or they miss the last wheel as they try to get back on the end of the paceline. Strong riders need to fill these gaps in order to preserve the flow, even if it means jumping across and moving back up the line early.

○ Reduce your effort up hills because the draft is less. Conversely, accelerate more quickly on descents so that everyone won't stack up from behind.

Hot Tips for High Temps

BEAT THE HEAT

By Fred Matheny

To prepare for the Atlanta Olympics, U.S. cyclists were backed by the power of Project 96—a high-tech Olympic program that brought together coaches, sports scientists, and other experts to refine everything from each rider's nutrition to track-team aerodynamics. The result was a greater understanding of cycling performance, if not a load of medals. But what does Olympian knowledge mean to average riders?

Plenty. The improvements that helped the national team compete against the world's best cyclists can also help you. One aspect that received lots of research was how heat and humidity affect cycling performance. Atlanta's hot, muggy summer climate guaranteed conditions that only a ripening Georgia peach could love. What Project 96 learned can help any rider cope in meltdown conditions.

LESSONS FROM "HOTLANTA"

The importance of being prepared to cope with heat is underscored when you realize that humans are wet creatures, little more than water in a sack. This is noted by Arnie Baker, M.D., a *Bicycling* magazine fitness advisory board member and several-time masters national champion, who says that each of us "contains about 40 quarts of fluids and about 5 quarts of blood."

The loss of this fluid occurs quickly in high temperatures. It's possible to sweat out more than 2 quarts per hour, and a fluid loss of 8 percent of body weight can occur in just a few hours. Humidity accelerates the process because evaporative cooling slows.

When you're as little as a quart or two low, your ability to sweat is reduced and body temperature rises. This leads to poor performance—

loss of speed and endurance. In fact, a South African study shows that fluid losses of as little as 2 percent of body weight significantly reduce high-intensity cycling time from start to exhaustion.

Some of the solutions include special nutrition and clothing that helps dissipate heat, says Edmund R. Burke, Ph.D., associate professor of exercise science at the University of Colorado in Colorado Springs, an exercise physiologist who has worked with the U.S. national cycling team since the mid-1970s, and the coordinator of Project 96. The U.S. cyclists experimented with glycerol, a legal substance that increases the body's ability to store water. Glycerol, available at some health food and sports specialty stores, is ingested before an event along with an ample amount of liquid, then you drink a lower concentration to maintain the effect as the event wears on. Tolerance is highly individual, however, with the amount necessary for effectiveness causing nausea in some riders. If you want to try glycerol, do so in training to find out how your body reacts before risking it in an event.

Beyond glycerol and special fabrics, our Olympic riders also adhered to a basic program of heat relief. This is advice everyone can follow.

Drink plenty of fluids. Hydrate before, during, and after rides. Practice drinking more than you want. "Thirst is inadequate to stimulate complete rehydration in a cyclist," warns Dr. Baker. "Learn to drink fluids before you are thirsty—at least a quart prior to competition and at least 4 ounces every 15 minutes during cycling."

Long-distance riders should consider using a hydration system, especially in areas where there may be lengthy periods between opportunities to refill bottles. Hydration systems let you carry as much as 90 ounces in a "bladder" worn like a backpack. A convenient hose dangles over your shoulder, letting you sip frequently. Competitive century riders also like these systems because stopping to fill bottles may mean losing contact with a fast group.

Don't cut back when using sports drinks. Paradoxically, these superfuels sometimes reduce hydration because cyclists think that they don't have to drink as much if they are consuming one. And the sweet, sticky taste (especially when a drink gets warm in a bike bottle) also stops some riders from drinking enough.

"Electrolyte loss is less important than fluid loss," says Dr. Baker. So if you can't swallow enough sports drink to stay chemically replenished, don't forget plain water. Some riders carry a bottle of water and another filled with sports drink, sipping them alternately.

To keep liquids cool and palatable, freeze half a bottle of sports drink overnight, then top it off before the ride. "Cooler drinks are better tolerated, which means you're more apt to drink enough," says Dr. Burke.

Weigh yourself. "Most of your weight loss reflects fluid loss, not fat loss," says Dr. Baker. "If you are down 2 pounds after a hot ride, that means you're down about a quart of liquid." Watch for persistent weight loss over several days or a week of hot-weather riding. It is a danger signal that you're becoming chronically dehydrated. To counteract this, carry a water bottle with you whenever you're off the bike and sip on it frequently.

Dress right. You might not have access to the Olympic team's special high-tech materials or secret weaves, but you probably do have light-colored cycling apparel. Wear it. Light colors reflect sunlight instead of absorbing it, keeping you cooler. For the same reason wear a well-ventilated white helmet rather than one of a darker color. Other real-person tips: Mesh jerseys are cooler than tightly woven ones. Also look for shorts made from wicking materials such as Ultrasensor, Aloft, or Tactel. These materials are less clammy in high humidity and help sweat evaporate quicker to enhance cooling.

Wear your helmet. Cyclists once used heat as an excuse to leave helmets at home. But several studies have shown that modern, well-vented helmets are actually as cool as a bare head because they funnel breezes onto the scalp's surface. Also, helmet material has a "beer cooler" effect, insulating the head from the heat.

Coat exposed areas. Although one study indicated that some skin damage occurs even when skin is protected with sunscreen rated as high as sun protection factor (SPF) 22, it's still a good idea to daub some on exposed areas. In fact, researchers at Oregon State University in Corvallis found that cyclists wearing sunscreen have skin temperatures up to 20 percent lower than those without. This is because sunscreen moisturizes skin and helps cool it through convection—the same type of cooling you feel when you turn on the fan during indoor training.

How to Prepare for Winter

CONQUER THE COLD

By Davis Phinney

Summer may be the most fun time to ride, but winter supplies the stories. I remember one spell at home in Boulder, Colorado, when the mercury stayed below zero for days. (Check the "Windchill Chart" on page 54 to see how cold that becomes when creating a 20-mile-per-hour headwind on the bike.) But I was facing a long, tough spring in the European pro peloton, so I had to get the miles in. One morning, teammate Andy Hampsten and I decided that we should fly someplace warmer or get out and ride. We rode.

The day was bone-chilling. We wore ski goggles and had layers of polypropylene, wool, and windproofing. We climbed out of town and immediately felt overdressed. Only 20 minutes into the ride, we stopped to shed a layer and found that our bottles were frozen solid. We prepared to descend the canyon back to Boulder by stuffing plastic bags from a garbage can down the length of our tights. Occasionally, I stopped to run with my bike, trying to promote circulation.

At one point a guy in a car offered us a lift. "No thanks," Hampsten shouted. "We're fine."

A few months later, in freakish blizzard conditions, Hampsten would take the overall lead on the Gavia Pass and go on to become the first North American to win the Giro d'Italia. Sometimes those epic training rides pay off.

PREPARING YOUR BODY AND YOUR BIKE

The first rule of cold-weather riding is to dress in layers. Use fabrics with good moisture-transfer capability so that sweat can dissipate to the outside and leave your skin relatively dry. No longer should you settle for cotton (poor wicking capacity) or wool (insulates well, stays wet forever). Polypropylene base layers are good, but Pearl Izumi has developed what it claims is a better fabric. They even named this proprietary material after me—Phintec.

After the base layer, don a synthetic jersey, preferably fleece. I use a windproof vest to keep my core warm, then put a jacket over that, which is easy to remove. Carry a foldable, waterproof shell if there is any chance of precipitation.

Legs don't need layers, but always wear warmers or tights when the temperature is below 65°F. Don't be macho about wearing shorts in cold weather. Your knees and muscles will suffer.

Take care of your extremities. Wear two thin cycling socks instead of one thick pair (which may make your shoes fit too tight and cut off circulation). Buy your shoe covers a little too large so that you can put a sock (with a hole cut for the cleat) over your shoe and under the cover. Wear gloves and take an extra pair in case the others get wet. Use liners inside for extra insulation against the chill of long descents. It's hard to brake with full mittens, but split-finger gloves work well. These have one compartment for your thumb, one for your first two fingers, and a third for your ring and pinkie fingers. This design pools heat almost as well as mittens.

Cover your neck by making one of the layers a turtleneck shirt or wear a neck gaiter or bandanna. A balaclava or wide headband holds heat under your helmet. Use a weatherproof helmet cover if too much heat is still escaping.

Check your bike before a long, cold ride—especially the tires. Fix-

WINDCHILL CHART

Wind (mph)	Temperature (°F)									
0	35	30	25	20	15	10	5	0	-5	-10
	Equivalent Temperature (°F)									
5	32	27	22	16	11	6	0	-5	-10	-15
10	22	16	10	3	-3	-9	-15	-22	-27	-34
15	16	9	2	-5	-11	-18	-25	-31	-38	-45
20	12	4	-3	-10	-17	-24	-31	-39	-46	-53
25	8	1	-7	-15	-22	-29	-36	-44	-51	-59
30	6	-2	-10	-18	-25	-33	-41	-49	-56	-64
35	4	-4	-12	-20	-27	-35	-43	-52	-58	-67
40	3	-5	-13	-21	-29	-37	-45	-53	-60	-69

ing a flat is a minor inconvenience in summer but a potential disaster in winter. Even 5 minutes of standing around can give you a severe chill that you can't shake. A stiff link is a major pain to fix in freezing temps, so keep your chain lubed. Be sure your spokes are evenly tensioned and your fenders are tight and secure.

Although rainy-day preparations aren't as extensive as those on cold days, there is one important rule to remember: Get fenders. In the rainy Northwest they are mandatory. I never knew the joy of wet riding until I trained in Vancouver, where all the riders had fenders. Up there, you're not welcome in a group unless your fenders are adequate. It's the water splashing up from the road that really makes wet riding unpleasant.

TIPS FOR WINTER RIDING

Here are some tips to ensure that your winter rides are safe, comfortable, and productive.

O Ride with a friend or group. Sharing conversation as well as a draft helps the miles go by. But group rides must be cohesive. Don't let them degenerate into hammerfests. You shouldn't do any hard, fast riding when the temperature is below 50°F. You'll feel sluggish, and it's difficult to generate leg speed. Instead, use winter to accumulate base miles.

O Head into the wind to start each ride. Get it out of the way early when you're still fresh. If you work up a sweat, having a tailwind on the return trip will decrease the chill. A headwind will make it much worse.

O Don't overdress. If you're not chilly in the first few minutes, you have probably worn too much and will overheat.

O In freezing temperatures start with hot drinks and use insulated bottles or bottle covers to increase the time before liquids turn to slush.

O Be wary of shaded corners, which may hide ice.

O Wear light, bright colors to help motorists see you on dim days.

O Install rear reflectors or carry reflective ankle bands for times when dusk catches you a few minutes from home.

○ Carry two tubes. Patching a tube with freezing fingers isn't easy, should a second flat occur.

○ Don't stop for long, if at all. Resumption of the windchill will make you cold, and you may be unable to shake the shivers for the rest of the ride.

○ Don't overdo it. As a rule, you can be fairly comfortable for 90 minutes in subfreezing temperatures. But things may deteriorate quickly after that, particularly if you have raised a sweat.

○ Take time to recover after riding. Winter takes more out of you. Because of the elements and your lower fitness level, a 50-mile winter ride feels like 80 miles.

○ Be extra careful when you have been sick. Don't try to make up a week of lost training by hammering before you are completely well. There is plenty of time to get back on track when spring arrives.

○ If you live where winters are mild, you still need to go easy. Use winter for recovery. Don't get caught in the flying-in-January, dead-by-June trap.

RAINY-DAY RISKS

By Davis Phinney

D oes riding on wet, slippery surfaces boost your heart rate faster than a sprint up a killer hill? Most people ride scared, especially when they have to lean through a turn. It certainly pays to be cautious, but you don't have to be chicken. I tried to use this outlook to my advantage when I was racing.

I remember one time in particular, in Austin, Texas. The rain was coming down steadily as we waited at the starting line. The gray pavement was turning black, and the road had an ugly, oily sheen. With six corners per lap on the slick criterium course, anticipation had given way to fear. The nervous tension was reflected in every face. I spent the whole race refining my line through the last two turns. Then, on the final lap, I leaned it over as far as I dared. I heard the rider directly behind me lose traction and slide away, but I stuck the last corner and had my arms up in a victory salute well before crossing the finish line.

Here are some pointers that will help you, too, corner confidently when the going gets wet.

Gain valuable experience. If practice doesn't make perfect, it at least makes you better. If you view every corner on every ride as an opportunity to practice cornering technique, your understanding of turning mechanics will get better. And once you understand the mechanics, your comfort zone will expand and your confidence will soar.

First, choose a line that allows you to carve a smooth arc through the turn. Start wide, cut to the apex, then swing wide again. Shift your weight to the rear of the saddle, put the outside pedal down and weight it, then lean the bike into the turn with gentle pressure on the inside of the handlebar. Practice on a grass field using traffic cones, then in a parking lot, and finally on the road.

WET-WEATHER WISDOM

Here are some additional things to remember on a rainy ride.

○ Water reduces the brake pads' friction on the rims. Apply the brakes to both wheels well before you need to slow or stop so that the moisture is squeegeed away. As soon as it is, the brakes may suddenly grab. Be ready to lighten your grip, or you may skid.

○ Beware of lane lines and other painted markers. When wet, these become much more slippery than unpainted blacktop because the plastic paint fills in the pavement's traction-producing irregularities. Plan your line so that you don't have to lean the bike much (if at all) on paint.

○ Wet metal objects, such as manhole covers and sewer grates, are even slicker than wet painted lines. Avoid them by looking ahead and carefully picking your line. Be very cautious on metal bridge surfaces and railroad tracks. Rain makes them as slick as ice. Sometimes the smart choice is to dismount and walk.

○ Wet leaves are very slippery, too, so beware in autumn. Try to avoid riding through puddles of which you can't see the bottom. There could be a pothole lurking underneath.

○ You can't ride if you can't see, so wear eye protection to keep raindrops (and grit thrown up in road spray) out of your eyes. Clear or yellow lenses let you see road details on the gloomiest of days. Avoid dark tints.

○ Rain and mist reduce motorists' vision, so help them see you by dressing in bright colors. Never wear a dull-hued rain jacket, which works like camouflage on a gloomy day. Instead, choose bright yellow, orange, or red. If the jacket has reflective stripes or piping, so much the better.

—Fred Matheny

Lean the bike gently. Don't dive into wet corners. The first rule I teach is that the bike will turn, if leaned. How much you lean depends on the turn's tightness, your speed, and the available traction. Although wet roads don't automatically mean less traction, always assume that they do. On slick turns you don't want to push the bike over too far because you may slide out. Conversely, I find that the oft-recommended method of holding the bike upright while leaning the body out into the turn isn't necessary either. The best method in the wet is to maintain an even angle with both bike and body leaning over together. In this way you let the bike turn instead of trying to make it turn.

Remain calm. Easier said than done, right? Think of driving a car. In poor conditions a death grip on the wheel will cause you to creep along, and in an emergency it will increase your chances of ending up in the ditch. Similarly, on two wheels, tension magnifies any mistake. So consciously let your tension go. Try exhaling as you approach a turn (wet or dry). Feel your shoulders drop and your grip lighten.

Use light movements. Braking evenly between the front and rear wheel will help you stay in control and keep the tires planted. Ease off the brakes as you enter the turn. (If necessary, you can continue to feather the rear brake.) Pretend that you're a stream of water finding a smooth path around the corner. Flow like a river so that there is no jerky motion, only a seamless arc. Flow takes rhythm and a little soul. No slam dancing here. Pick a smooth, gradual line. Ideally, all motion is subtle, all reactions are soft.

RIDING AT NIGHT

By Ed Pavelka

Until you have ridden in the dark, you can't imagine the pleasures. Even familiar roads become new again when you're gliding along in your bubble of light. The air is cooler and cleaner, and the wind is usually calm. Because visibility is limited, you seem to hear more. The stars form a magical canopy. On a quiet back road you can even switch off your headlight to fully enjoy the ivory aura.

I have ridden hundreds of hours at night, most of them during commuting or long-distance events that started before daybreak and sometimes stretched past sunset. I still remember my apprehension the first time I climbed aboard a bike in the dark. But 15 minutes into that ride, my fears vanished. It was fun! My headlight let me see the road fine, and thanks to my taillight and several reflectors, overtaking drivers saw me in plenty of time. In fact, they slowed more and passed wider than they usually did in daylight.

There's no denying, though, that a high percentage of car/bike accidents happen at night. Often, the cyclist is at fault. You may notice these riders, darting through streets on bikes with no lights and few reflectors. Combine near-invisibility with risky riding practices, and the potential for disaster rises dramatically. That's why it pays to know about the equipment and techniques that reduce the threat.

SEE AND BE SEEN

Even if you ride where there are streetlights bright enough to show you the way, you still need a headlight. Why? Because it's the law in every state. Even when a headlight isn't necessary to see the road, it helps motorists and pedestrians see you.

For serious night riding, choose a dual-beam headlight with a rechargeable battery.

There are three types of headlights. Generator lights have fallen out of favor because they put drag on the bike and go out when you're not moving. Small battery-powered lights are reasonably priced and produce an adequate beam, so they're fine for riding under streetlights or for short distances in the dark. Cyclists serious about night riding, however, usually invest in the third type: dual-beam systems that run on a rechargeable nickel-cadmium or gel-cell battery. These systems are expensive (usually $175 or more) but require no additional battery purchases. The bright, dependable light enhances safety and inspires confidence. Burn times for most models are between 1 and 4 hours per charge, depending on how much the high beam is used.

Whether or not your state requires a taillight, it's a good idea to use one along with several reflectors. Inexpensive, battery-powered taillights are available from various companies. Most have light-emitting LEDs instead of bulbs, so their bright, penetrating beam can't burn out. Serious night riders should use two or more such taillights plus frame-mounted reflectors, pedal reflectors, and reflective tape. Reflective vests, jackets, and helmet covers are available, too. Make sure that some of these are on the sides of you or your bike so that they help at intersections. The idea is to look like a mobile version of the White House Christmas tree, sparkling so brightly that you catch the eye of every driver.

In case of bulb failure, carry spares and perhaps even a small battery-powered emergency headlight. This can also be used for bike repairs in the dark.

RIDING TECHNIQUES

Night is the same as day in terms of traffic laws and rules for safe cycling. Visibility is the big difference. All vehicles (bikes included) are best identified by the light they emit or reflect. This is another reason that it pays to go overboard. The quicker a driver notices you and identifies you as a cyclist, the better.

One potential danger is outriding your headlight. That is, going too fast to react quickly enough should something dangerous enter your beam. This is unlikely to happen if you have one of the premium rechargeable light systems—until you descend at high speed. Resist this temptation unless Russian roulette is your idea of an acceptable risk.

Wet roads also reduce the distance that you can see well. Your headlight beam glances off the shiny, smooth surface and diffuses, leaving the road darker and less defined than when it's dry. Combine this reduced visibility with the increased time it takes for brakes to work when wet, and the danger doubles.

If you are using a strong headlight, most oncoming drivers will dim their high beams for you. Even so, their lights can be dazzling out of the darkness. Never look into them; instead, watch the right edge of the road so that you can avoid being blinded and maintain a straight line. Some night riders use a visor on their helmet so they can tip their head to block oncoming headlights.

After dark there are fewer drivers on the road, which is one reason that night riding is enjoyable. But there is a greater percentage of drunk drivers. Be cautious on Friday and Saturday nights, especially on highways that pass through areas with bars and taverns. If the highway doesn't have a shoulder to ride on, find an alternate route.

Above all, ride defensively. That's always a good idea, but after dark be even more cautious, especially at intersections. In the mix of movement and lights, always assume that drivers don't see you even when you have the right of way. Then, when you are safely away from congestion, relax and enjoy being on your bike at night.

THREE

Safety in Traffic

STREET SMARTS

By Michael McGettigan

Cyclists hate riding in traffic. In surveys "dangerous traffic" consistently ranks as the top reason that cyclists don't commute more often or ride as much as they would like to in bigger cities.

It's understandable. Urban traffic can be a full-scale cycling assault. Pedestrians charge into your path. Hostile motorists bomb by in cars the size of tanks. And all the while, you're trying to navigate roads that have been battered by potholes or excavations. You can't change any of these factors, but you can alter your reaction to them. You can learn to ride more safely and smoothly in even the worst rush-hour traffic.

I know plenty of riders who can hammer me into the ground but don't know how to execute a simple one-footed curb climb. Here are some tips for doing that—and a whole lot more.

Practice. Pedal between parked cars at malls or supermarkets to get used to having all that metal around. This will help you feel comfortable when drivers simply pass normally. Save your adrenaline for true emergencies.

Look ahead. Don't worry excessively about the traffic behind you. New urban warriors fear getting hit from the rear, but this isn't the most common collision. The majority (about 25 percent) of city car/bike accidents happen when driver and rider cross each other's path at intersections and driveways—especially when a driver turns in front of a rider.

Recruit a pro. Have an experienced road warrior accompany you on your first ride, alternately leading and following. When you're in back, try to determine why he is doing what he's doing. When you're in front, try to do what he did and listen for shouted advice. There is no better way to learn the basic rules and intricacies of city cycling.

Stay on the straight and narrow. Learn how to look behind you without swerving. This is a key skill for surviving busy streets. Practice riding straight on the painted lines of quiet roads or parking lots. Once you can do this, try maintaining your course while turning your head to the left. Slightly drop your left shoulder while keeping your right shoulder level. Don't rely on peripheral vision. You should be able to turn your head far enough to make actual eye contact.

Still can't do it? Try this trick: Stick out your left arm straight behind you, then turn your head, shoulders, and neck as you look over your left shoulder. Sighting down your arm will help you ride straight. Eventually, you'll be able to do it without using your arm as a guide.

Get noticed. Drivers don't actively ignore cyclists. They are just cued to spot larger objects. They also mistake us for pedestrians at first glance and don't expect us to be moving very fast.

To be recognized for what you are, you must get drivers to look twice. Shake your head at them, wiggle your handlebar (but not enough to cause instability), and use body English on your bike. This helps you register in their peripheral vision and also helps indicate your direction. Watch messengers and other experienced city commandos. They are smooth and stable but not so silky that they drop off the screen for drivers.

Lighten up. Outfit yourself and your bike so that you can be seen. Bright-colored gloves get attention because they are so often in motion, says Louise Kornreich, a bike messenger in Seattle. Your helmet is another potential eye-catcher. Put as much reflective material on your helmet—and your bike frame—as you can bear. And from dusk to dawn, use a headlight with side visibility and a strong taillight. In fact, there is evidence that seeing two front-mounted lights helps drivers estimate speed and distance better than seeing a single light.

Go with the flow. In normal situations ride in the right lane, but as far to the left as is practical. This puts you farther out in the traffic flow, but it's safer. Drivers won't be tempted to squeeze past you. It also reduces the risk of getting nailed when someone flings open the door of a parked car. Claim the entire lane, if that's what you need to ensure safety. Don't move to the right at intersections or when a long string of parking spaces is empty. You'll just have to push back into traffic repeatedly, perhaps popping unexpectedly into a driver's view. Stay out there where you belong.

Assume the position. Use your position within the lane to signal your intentions. When you are preparing to merge or turn left, move to the left part of the lane. Stay center when you are traveling straight at cruising speed—that is, as fast as the flow of traffic. Move right when you want to merge or turn in that direction or to permit cars to pass. (That's right, permit. As you move to the side, wave them around. You are training them to work with us rather than push us out of the way.)

Chart your course. Practice the SIPDE (scan, identify, predict, decide, execute) method taught by the Motorcycle Safety Foundation.

○ Scan the street (and sidewalk) ahead.

○ Identify potential hazards.

○ Predict their movements.

○ Decide on a course of action.

○ Execute the maneuver that takes you safely along your chosen line.

Continuously split your attention among your immediate line through traffic, your escape route (an alternate line in case your path is blocked), side streets, and any traffic you have passed that might overtake you later. Don't get distracted by any vehicles, sounds, or events outside your line. Just note them and decide if they will enter your line later. This takes a lot of practice at first. Eventually, it becomes instinct.

Know your cues. The big picture has many scenes. When you see a guy hailing the cab that has been poking along behind you, it means that the yellow menace could soon roar past and turn in any direction— probably without signaling. Likewise, a pedestrian hesitating to cross a side street may have spotted someone who is going to try to beat the traffic light. Maybe it's just a bike messenger. Maybe it's a 10-ton truck. Either way, it will soon come roaring into your path.

Check out the dashboard of the car alongside you to see if either turn signal is flashing. A driver who doesn't use his signals may still give notice of his intentions by the angle of his head or the car's wheels. In heavy traffic scan two or more cars ahead for exhaust smoke (indicating acceleration or deceleration) and "shivers" (indicating potholes and other rough spots).

Eye oncoming traffic. Don't get picked off when a car coming from the opposite direction turns left. This can happen when you trail a string of autos through an intersection. The opposing driver times his turn for after the last car. He might not see you. Stick close to that last car, even pulling alongside it. Or slow and be prepared to brake.

Make a left the right way. The same principle applies when you want to make a left. You're less likely to get hit by an oncoming car if you stay close to the car in front of you through the turn. If there isn't one, brake and wait for an opening.

Avoid a squeeze play. Drivers will try to sneak past you, then cut you off to turn right. You can tell what they are up to because they usually drift toward the left side of the lane as they approach the intersection, setting up for the quick turn. After a while, you will be able to sense them and stay centered in the lane to make them wait for you. Or you can just slow and stay out of their way. Your call.

Watch for blind spots. Drivers test for openings in traffic by nosing their cars out of driveways and side streets with limited visibility. When you approach such spots, stand tall on the pedals and try to make eye contact. Take the center of the lane and check for escape space to the left.

Slide by slippery surfaces. City streets are dotted with oil and transmission fluid. Oil tends to gather in the middle of the road (where the drips fall), so keep to one side even when you're riding the center of the lane. Steel repair plates and painted road markers also become treacherous when wet. If you find yourself on a slippery surface, straighten the bike, level the pedals to the 3 and 9 o'clock positions, don't brake, keep your elbows and knees flexed, and let momentum carry you through.

Learn all the right moves. Climbing parallel curbs is one of the most useful skills for city cycling, whether you're escaping an auto or merely bringing your bike onto the sidewalk as you reach your destination. Angle toward the curb, leaving the inside pedal (the one closest to the curb) down at the 6 o'clock position. As your front wheel reaches the curb, swing your foot off the low pedal and onto the sidewalk. Your back wheel should be about 1 to 2 feet from the curb. Step forward, putting your weight on the foot that's planted on the sidewalk. Hoist your front wheel onto the sidewalk as you pedal with the other foot to bring the back wheel up and over the curb.

Size up your cycle. Many new riders get wedged between cars or freeze when they could ride through a gap. You should know how big your bike is. Measure it at its widest point. Play games (at low speed) to see if you can fit between that mailbox and parking meter. Get an idea of how long you are, too. Learn your limits before a crisis.

Be prepared. Whenever you stop, be ready for an emergency take-off. Keep your foot on the high pedal while you check behind. If that bus driver doesn't notice you, you want to be able to move—fast.

Customize for urban rides. You can "citify" your bike by raising your handlebar and lowering your seat slightly for better visibility and hop-ability. To reduce flats, run slightly beefier tires, Kevlar-belted tires, or self-sealing tubes. Invest in a bell, a lock, fenders, and a rack and bungee cords.

Here are three other add-ons that new riders probably wouldn't think of (but shouldn't be without).

○ A bandanna comes in handy for wiping your face, hands, and bike. Have one for every day of the week.

○ A disposable shower cap is perfect for covering the saddle when you park your bike outdoors in the rain. You can store the cap under your seat.

○ A mesh bag takes up practically no room but holds your helmet, light, seat, gloves, and more in a single, easy-to-carry package. It's also good for hanging up cycling clothes to dry at the office.

Develop good timing. Learn to ride the rhythms of the city. One of the most powerful is "the pulse," a series of timed traffic signals that creates a solid mass of vehicles catching synchronized green lights. Strong riders may feel exhilarated surfing a roaring wave of cars. If you don't enjoy the pulse, pedal only on untimed, more leisurely streets. It's also possible to ride a timed street between pulses, pulling aside at intersections to let the mob pass, then pedaling along in the empty spaces. Don't let traffic force you into meaningless sprints to red lights.

Steer smart. When you exceed 5 miles per hour, countersteering is the best way to execute a quick, evasive swoop around a small road hazard or to curve inside a turning car's radius when you're cut off at a corner. This technique makes even a clunker agile because it uses the bike's own weight and wheels to start the turn.

To execute a countersteer, push your handlebar left to start a right turn or right to start a left turn. Sounds strange? Well, you steer a bike by leaning. Pushing your bar just makes the bike start the lean sequence quickly. Then steer back and sweep around the obstacle.

Be aware of your own lean angle. Many cyclists lean their bikes and not their bodies. This widens your turning radius and lessens the countersteer. Also, make sure that you don't zip into traffic when you countersteer. Better a pothole than a Pontiac.

Navigate obstacles. When you can't avoid road hazards such as potholes, ride over them as lightly as possible. An experienced rider can usually bunnyhop an obstacle by pressing down on the handlebar to compress the front tire, then lifting up on the bar and curling it forward while pulling up on the pedals. If you can do it, more power to you.

For beginners here's a safe way to do it. Level your pedals as you approach the obstacle. Just before impact, lift the front of the bike, or at least take your weight off it. When the front clears, lean forward to take your weight off the rear wheel. Pedal away. Use the same technique for hopping a curb head-on (not parallel to you).

To safely move from the curb to the street, reverse the process. Level your pedals. Lean back on the seat as your front wheel drops over the curb. Then lean onto the bar when the front wheel touches down. If the curb is high, hop lightly off the pedals as the back of the bike drops down to street level. Be sure that clearing a curb doesn't distract you from traffic.

Respect pedestrians. One reality of city riding is that you will sometimes use the sidewalk. Remember that it is not your place; you are a guest. Don't bring the rush of street riding over the curb. When passing, don't ring, whistle, or shout within 5 feet of pedestrians. Their brains need more time to process data. Otherwise, all you're doing is scaring them. And don't dog them, riding on their heels until they let you pass. This is obnoxious.

Keep it clean. When you walk your bike, be aware of where the chain and other dirty bits are in relation to pedestrians. Chainring "tattoos" are even less cool when you're not a cyclist.

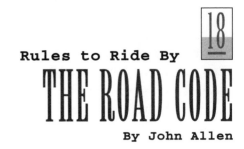

Rules to Ride By
THE ROAD CODE

By John Allen

We have all seen cyclists who wander across the road, who go from the sidewalk to the street, who weave in and out between parked cars. From moment to moment, nobody can tell what these riders will do next. Pedestrians jump back. Drivers stomp on their brakes.

On the other hand, we have seen cyclists who seem to blend into the traffic flow smoothly and effortlessly. You always know where they are headed, and you feel comfortable around them—whether you're on a bicycle, in a car, or on foot. They make riding in traffic look easy. What are their techniques for doing it right?

CHOOSING SIDES

With very few exceptions, the safest way to ride in traffic is to act like traffic. Go with the normal flow. Cyclists who ride this way get where they're going faster and, according to accident studies, have about five times fewer mishaps than riders who make up their own rules.

Generally, the more you follow normal traffic patterns, the more predictable and safer you are. The rules of the road establish a way to behave in every situation. Sometimes a cyclist has to wait for drivers—at a stop sign, for example—but sometimes it's the drivers who have to wait. The rules of the road protect you by making it clear what should happen next for every vehicle.

Riding right begins with riding on the right. Unknowing cyclists think that they are safer on the left, where they can see cars coming. But riding on the left is a primary cause of car/bike accidents.

If you ride in violation of this basic traffic rule, you greatly increase your risk of an accident. You also give up all your rights. If you are on the left and an accident occurs, a court will almost always find you at fault.

Also, if you ride against the flow of traffic, you and an oncoming car approach each other at the sum of your respective speeds. If you are going 15 miles per hour and the car is going 35 miles per hour, the closing speed is 50 miles per hour. But if you are riding on the right with the flow of traffic, the difference in speed is only 20 miles per hour. That means a driver behind you has much more time to react. Also, drivers and pedestrians about to emerge from side streets and crosswalks will be looking toward you, in the direction traffic normally comes from.

LIVING ON THE EDGE

Normally, slower traffic keeps to the right, and faster traffic passes on the left. Because your bicycle is slower than other traffic, you should ride near the right edge of the road. But how far to the right should you be?

The usable width of the road begins where you can ride without increased danger of falls, jolts, or blowouts. A road may have a gravel shoulder, its edge may be covered with sand or trash, or the pavement may be broken. Don't ride there. You will usually find better pavement about 12 to 18 inches to the left of the road edge where it's swept clean of sand and debris by passing traffic. For a cyclist the right edge of the road begins here.

Most bicycle accidents are simple falls due to either rider error or road hazards. Train your eyes to scan the scene ahead. Keep them moving. Look up at traffic and also down at the road for potholes and debris.

Ride far enough into the lane to avoid creating blind spots. If you ride too close to parked cars on your right, you can't see around them into side streets and driveways. A pedestrian, car, or bike could come out from between them. Drivers on side streets might nose their cars into your path to check for traffic. The door of a parked car could swing open in front of you.

Where there are parked cars, the usable width of the street begins about 3 feet to the left of them. The same goes for a wall, a hedge, or another obstruction. As you approach a blind intersection or driveway, you should be even farther from the road edge. Imagine the front of a car suddenly protruding into your path. Avoid this danger zone.

Don't dart into the spaces between parked cars. If you weave to the right after passing a parked car, it will hide you from drivers approaching from behind. Then you have to pop back out when you reach the next parked car. Put yourself in the place of a driver a couple of hundred feet back. Could this driver see you before you suddenly reappear?

Sure, many people—even some cycling "experts"—will tell you to "always ride as far to the right as possible" and "watch for opening car doors." But at speeds above 5 miles per hour, you can't stop in time to avoid a car door. Your only choice is to swerve into the street—maybe into the path of a passing car. Motorists don't mind slowing for a competent, predictable cyclist nearly as much as they mind slamming the brakes for a rider swerving in front of them.

RIDING WIDE LANES

If the road has a paved shoulder or an extra-wide right lane, don't ride all the way over at the right edge. Instead, follow a straight line 3 to 4 feet to the right of the cars in the right lane. Stay a constant distance from the painted line that marks the boundary of the right lane.

If you ride at the far right edge of the shoulder, you're much more likely to be cut off by a right-turning car. If this should happen, it's harder for you to avoid an accident. By the time you see the car, it will be blocking your path. If you're closer to the car, you can turn with it and avoid hitting its side.

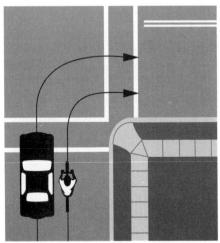

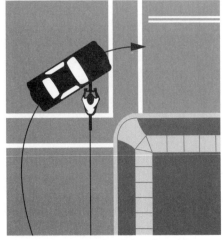

In a wide lane you are safer if you stay just to the right of traffic so that you can turn quickly to avoid an accident.

If you ride on the far right of a wide lane, a turning car might cut you off before you see it.

There is one important exception to this rule: In several states it's legal for bicyclists to ride on high-speed limited-access highways. Here, you should ride at the right edge of the shoulder to avoid the wind blast from big trucks. Except at on- or off-ramps, limited-access highways have no cross-traffic, so there's no risk from turning cars or pedestrians.

ARE YOU NARROW-MINDED?

In a wide lane there is room for cars to pass you. But in a narrow lane cars have to move partway into the opposing lane. Narrow lanes are common on city streets and country roads.

On a narrow two-lane road, stay alert for strings of cars coming at you in case one suddenly pulls into your lane to pass. Ride near the edge if cars are coming from only one direction at a time. Then cars from the rear can get around you without having to move as far into the other lane.

But if cars are coming from both directions, you have to take control of the situation. You can't risk letting a driver pass you in the face of oncoming traffic. There's simply no room. Glance behind, then take the first opportunity to move to the middle of your lane.

Also, merge to the middle of a narrow right lane for a blind curve, where there might be oncoming traffic. This makes you visible earlier to drivers coming from behind. They will have to slow and follow you. It helps to make a "slow" signal (left arm extended downward, open hand facing to the rear). This indicates that you're aware of the car behind and that it's unsafe to pass. Don't let an impatient driver cause an accident.

Understand that the law is on your side. You have the same right to use the road as a motorist, and this sometimes means making other traffic slow down for you. Because you don't have eyes in the back of your head, you can't be expected to keep track of traffic behind you. The driver approaching from the rear is required to slow and follow if it's not possible to pass safely.

It may seem dangerous to make a car slow for you, but it's not. The usual reason cyclists feel unsafe on narrow roads is that they don't take control of the situation. Remember that the drivers behind you don't have room to pass safely anyway. If you ride along the right edge, you're inviting them to try—and probably squeeze you off the road. If you show clearly that it's not safe for drivers to pass, it's unlikely that they will.

But be courteous. When it becomes safe to pass, give the driver a wave-by signal. If conditions are causing you to block traffic for more than a short time, the law requires you to pull to the side to let it by.

On a road with two or more narrow lanes in your direction (like many city streets), you should ride in the middle of the right lane at all times. Make drivers move to the passing lane to get by you. If you ride along the right edge, two cars may pass you simultaneously, side by side—a dangerous situation for you and the drivers.

THE PERFECT PASS

Usually, cars travel faster than bicycles. But not always. Perhaps a row of cars has slowed because of congestion. Or maybe you're riding down a hill as fast as the traffic flow.

If you're going the same speed, pull into line with the cars. When riding down a hill at high speed, you need more room to steer and brake. Besides, it's dangerous to ride beside a car. The driver, unaware that you're there, could turn right or squeeze you into the curb.

As long as you can keep up with the car in front, stay in line with it. If you begin to fall behind, pull to the right. If you want to pass, do it on the left, just as if you were driving a car. First, look back for traffic to make sure that you can pull safely into the passing lane. Signal your intention by extending your left arm. Keep your distance from the side of the car. Put yourself where the driver will look for you. If you're passing a big truck or bus, use even more clearance (5 to 6 feet) because it could move over before you can get out of its way. When you're clear, signal by extending your right arm and move back into the right lane.

Sometimes the vehicle that you're passing will pick up speed while you're still next to it. If this happens, maintain your position in the lane and brake lightly, if necessary, to fall back. Wait for an opening, then signal and merge to your normal position in the right lane.

A cyclist's place on the road follows accepted rules, the same as for motorists: Stay to the right when moving slowly, pull to the left to pass. The way you carry out these rules is a little different because your bicycle is narrow and usually slow. Now that you know how, you're ready to blend smoothly and safely into the traffic flow.

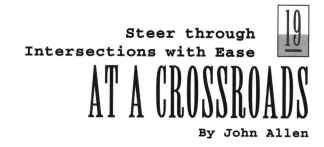

Steer through
Intersections with Ease

AT A CROSSROADS

By John Allen

Intersections are where all of your traffic-riding skills come together. If you can ride through intersections smoothly and confidently, you can handle almost any cycling situation.

The basics are simple. Move to the correct lane position depending on which way you want to go (right, left, or straight ahead). This may mean leaving your normal position near the right side of the road. If you're turning right, keep to the right. If you're turning left, move to the center of the road. If you're going straight, go between the right- and left-turning traffic.

KNOW YOUR RIGHTS

Right turns are easiest. Just stay in the right lane, check for traffic, signal by extending your right arm, and go around the corner. To avoid being squeezed against the curb of a narrow road by a car trying to pass, ride in the middle of the right lane. Remember that the rear of a car moves to the right as it makes a right turn.

At a stop sign or a traffic light where you can legally turn right on red, yield to through-traffic coming from the left. You're also required to yield to pedestrians on crosswalks. Cyclists are obligated to follow the same rules as drivers.

LOOK BACK, LOOK AHEAD

You need to change lane position for some intersection maneuvers. In fact, for some left turns you must move across more than one lane. This technique begins with looking back for traffic. Because your sense of balance is in your head, you should practice turning your head without swerving.

Some riders change lane position without looking back because they're afraid of swerving. Don't trust your ears. Many cars are very quiet, and a cyclist behind you is even quieter. Even if you use a rearview mirror, you must still glance back. A mirror will show you traffic that is directly behind you but not vehicles at your side.

Practice by riding along a painted straight line in an empty parking lot. Turn your head to glance back, then look forward again to see if you're still riding straight. To reduce swerving, slightly dip the shoulder you're looking over and think about your arm position. If you don't pull the handlebar, you won't swerve. Some riders who use low positions even duck their heads and look under their arms. Find the technique that works well for you, considering your riding posture and flexibility. Practice looking over both shoulders until maintaining a straight line is ingrained.

Now that you have checked behind, what next? If there is a car close, let it pass and deal with the next one. That driver will have time to react to your signals. If you make your intentions clear, you will almost always be permitted to move into the lane.

Extend your left arm to signal your wish to move left. Wait a couple of seconds, then look back again to check that the driver has slowed down or moved aside to make room.

Turning your head to look back is a signal, too. In slow, crowded traffic you need to keep your hands on the handlebar, ready to brake. You can usually move into line with the cars after signaling with a turn of your head. Make sure that the driver has made room for you. Most will, but there is no guarantee. It's not your signal that makes it safe to change lanes. It's the driver's acceptance of your signal.

If you begin your lane change early enough to deal with two drivers, you will almost always succeed. If the first one doesn't make room, the second one almost certainly will. In high-speed highway traffic, though, drivers may not have time to react. Then you need to wait for a gap big enough for moving across all lanes at once.

GO LEFT, YOUNG MAN (OR WOMAN)

To prepare for a left turn, change lanes until you reach the road's left-turn position. This is where no cars on your left will go straight—all will turn left. If the lane carrying left-turning traffic also carries through-traffic, ride at its left side. If it's a left-turn-only lane, ride at

Changing lanes is a two-step process: First, you cross the lane line, then you move to the other side of the lane.

its right side. On an ordinary two-lane street, be just to the right of the center line.

It may seem dangerous to move to the middle of the street, but this is the best position for a left turn. It puts all the traffic you have to deal with in front of you. Because you're to the left of the through-traffic coming from behind, you don't have to look back before turning. You can concentrate on the traffic from the left, right, and front.

If you have to cross more than one lane to reach the left-turn position, do it in steps. First, cross the lane line so that you are just inside the next lane. Second, cross to the far side of the lane. At each step look back and signal drivers to make room for you.

Yield to traffic entering the intersection. You can roll slowly forward the way cars do so that you're able to move fast when there's a gap in the traffic. Pass an oncoming left-turning vehicle right side to right side.

When turning left from the left side of a lane, don't let left-turning cars behind you pass on your right. While waiting, make a "slow" signal with your right hand (arm extended downward, open hand facing to the rear). Ride straight ahead for a few feet as you enter the intersection, allowing left-turning cars behind you to pass on your left.

It's also okay to hop off your bike at the right side of the road, then make a left turn as a pedestrian. This way, you can turn left legally at a "no left turn" sign or avoid traffic situations that are beyond your abilities.

STAY STRAIGHT

It's usually easy to ride straight through an intersection. You may have to change lanes, but not many. The key is to make sure that right-turning traffic passes you on your right. Stay completely out of the right-turn-only lane. If there is a lane marked for right turns *and* through-traffic, ride near its left side. On a multi-lane road, you may have to move into the second or third lane from the curb to avoid right-turning traffic.

The most difficult intersection to ride straight through is on a small two-lane street. Why? Because traffic in the right lane could go in any of three directions—right, left, or straight. On a street with parallel parking, the empty space between the last parked car and the corner serves as a right-turn lane. Don't wander into this space. Stay in the traffic lane.

On a street without parking, pull a little farther into the lane to discourage right-turning drivers from passing you on the left and then cutting you off. When stopping at a light, it is considerate to position yourself far enough from the curb so that drivers can turn right on red. If they hesitate to roll through, wave them by with your right hand.

Four Ways to Steer Clear of Danger

EVASIVE MANEUVERS

By John Allen

A bicycle is very maneuverable, which is both good and bad. It's good because as your riding skills improve, quick reactions will help you avoid dangerous situations. It's bad because a simple mistake can cause a crash. Bikes tip over pretty easily.

One common error is not recognizing slippery or loose surfaces. Sand, gravel, snow, ice, leaves, oil, and wet manhole covers and painted road markings can all make controlling your bike difficult. If you can't avoid riding over these, be ready to brake or accelerate as the situation dictates. Also be ready to put a foot down for support.

Be especially wary of diagonal railroad crossings, trolley tracks, raised lane-line dots, and "lips" between road shoulders and travel lanes. Any of these can push your front wheel to the side, sweeping your bike out from under you. When you can't avoid them, cross them at as close to a right angle as possible.

Beware of steel-grid bridge decks. They will steer your bike parallel to the gridding, making balancing difficult. When they are wet, their danger is compounded by their slipperiness. It's smart to dismount and walk across or use the sidewalk.

Any bump, rock, or pothole more than an inch high can squash your tires flat against the rims, damaging the rims and blowing out the tubes. Steer around these hazards and keep your tires inflated to maximum pressure so that they can protect the wheels from impacts you can't avoid.

Here are four techniques that are musts in a road cyclist's repertoire. When you get good at these emergency maneuvers, you'll notice gains in security, confidence, and style. You'll feel more relaxed, the sign of an experienced rider who is ready for any danger the road presents.

Avoiding obstacles. Thanks to your bike's maneuverability, you can learn to handle challenging situations. Here's an example. Let's say that you are on a pleasant two-lane country road, just wide enough for cars to pass you in your lane. You look up at the scenery and then down at the road. There's a rock directly in front! You also hear a car just behind. You can't swerve left into traffic, and you don't want to swerve right onto gravel. What to do?

The "rock dodge" maneuver: Make your wheels weave around the rock while riding in a straight line. Just as you reach the rock, quickly steer left, then right to correct your balance, then straight again.

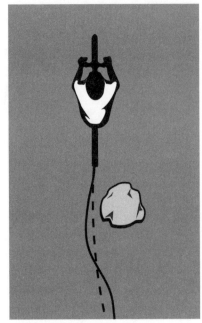

To avoid a rock, first turn the handlebar to one side, then correct your balance by quickly turning the other way.

Because you correct your balance quickly, your body doesn't have time to follow the bike's weave. You continue in a nearly straight line as you safely get around the hazard. To learn the rock dodge, go to an empty parking lot and practice until it becomes easy.

Turning quickly. Picture yourself in another pinch. You're riding down the street toward an intersection. A car on your left suddenly begins a right turn—and you're headed straight toward the car's side. To avoid hitting the car, you need to execute a sharp turn. But how?

Your bicycle balances the same way you balance a yardstick on the palm of your hand. If you want to quickly move the yardstick to the right, you move your hand to the left. Then the yardstick leans to the right, and you follow it with your hand.

Similarly, if you twitch your bike out from under you by steering to the left for an instant, you can then turn sharply to the right. The hard part is making yourself steer momentarily toward the car you're trying to avoid.

Practice this technique in your favorite parking lot. Going slowly at first, snap the handlebar quickly to the left. Your bike will lean to the right, and then you can steer right. As you get the hang of it, increase your speed. The faster you go, the less sharply you have to steer.

This "instant turn" technique is useful in many situations. If a car coming toward you begins a dangerous left turn, turn right onto the side street with it. If a car emerges from a side street on the right, turn onto the side street. It's best to turn to the right, behind the car. But if it's too late, turn left with the car. Even if you hit it, the closer you are to parallel, the lighter the impact will be.

Handling curves. Sooner or later you'll find yourself going around a downhill curve too fast. A variation on the instant turn can get you through this situation in one piece.

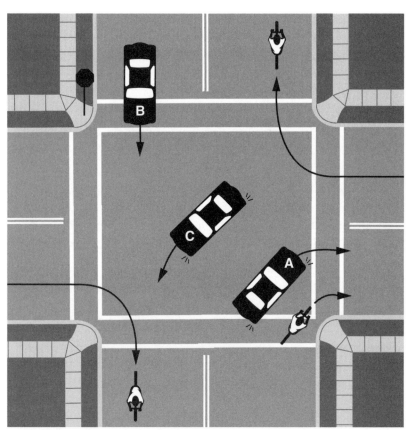

The "instant turn" technique can keep you out of harm's way. Use it to avoid (a) a right-turning car, (b) a car running a stop sign, and (c) a left-turning car. In each instance, you want to turn your bike to the right.

The usual panic reaction is to slam on the brakes. But this will straighten the bike and may send you headfirst off the road before you can stop. Instead, steer with the curve. Don't brake. Straighten the handlebar momentarily, as in an instant turn, to drop your bike into a deeper lean. Stand hard on the outside pedal. You'll be surprised how far you can angle your wheels without losing traction. But if you do slide down, you'll only skid on your side and come to a stop. That's much better than sailing across the road and perhaps hitting a car or guardrail head-on.

If you're about to ride into a wall or over a cliff, you may decide to deliberately slide down. Lean into the turn, then hit the brakes. The fall will hurt, but probably not as much as the alternative.

Hopping over hazards. There's a pothole straight ahead! No time for even a rock dodge. If only you could fly....

Well, you can for a little while—at least long enough to clear an obstacle like this. You need to hold the pedals horizontal, squat down, and prepare to pull on the handlebar. Spring up and yank your legs under you (assuming that you have toe clips and straps or a clipless pedal system). You'll be over the pothole faster than you can read "squat-pull-spring-yank."

Mountain biking has given us a new name for this maneuver: the bunnyhop. It was long known as just plain jumping. It's the quickest last-resort way to avoid a pothole or another road-surface hazard. Once you get good at it, you can even jump over low curbs or railroad tracks.

Practice in an empty parking lot. You must first lift the front wheel, then the rear wheel as it reaches the obstacle. The timing depends on how fast you're going. It's easier to clear objects at higher speeds because you cover more distance in the air.

Pedaling around the Rough Spots
SURVIVAL SKILLS

By John Allen

et's face it: Some traffic situations go beyond normal rules. When the system breaks down because of overcrowding, poor planning, or disrespect for the law, you may have to "bushwhack" your way through the mess. With care, you can emerge safely and maintain the respect of other road users. Here are some circumstances and places where you need to take the initiative.

Red lights. Always stop and wait at a red light. This not only ensures your safety but also increases respect for cyclists as law-abiding road users. But some traffic lights won't turn green until they receive a signal from a metal detector buried in the pavement. A bicycle doesn't have enough metal to make this gadget work all the time.

Recognize the detector by a square or octagonal pattern of thin grooves in the pavement. These are cut for sensor wires. The detector is most sensitive if the bike passes directly over one of the wires. Sometimes you can help by dismounting and laying the bike over a wire so there's more metal available. If nothing happens, you either have to wait for a car to arrive or proceed through the red light. You aren't breaking the law if the light isn't working.

Congested traffic. A traffic jam doesn't have to stop you. That's one of the biggest advantages of cycling in the city. But in the tight quarters of a tie-up, take extra care. Stopped cars in a traffic jam present the same hazards as parked cars: blind spots, doors, and unpredictable starts and turns.

If there is an open passing lane, use it rather than threading between cars. If the street is completely plugged, slowly pick your way forward with your hands on the brake levers. Remember, any car door could suddenly open.

In a total jam you can be fairly sure that cars won't move, because they have nowhere to go. But if there is an open driveway or a parking space into which a car could turn, you have to assume that it will. Look to see whether a car's front wheels are turned. Move away from the side of the car as you pass. Try to get the driver's attention as you approach the front of the car.

When cars are stopped but aren't completely bumper to bumper, watch out for drivers from other lanes darting into the gaps. Stop and look before you move into a gap yourself. Be especially careful if the vehicle you are passing doesn't have a hood you can see over.

Don't pass a long truck or bus stuck in a traffic jam unless there's an open lane next to it. As you ride close to the side of such a vehicle, it may begin to merge in your direction, leaving you no way to escape.

When you approach an intersection, change lanes to take the same position that you would in normal traffic. Before you cross in front of a car, make eye contact with the driver—even if the car is stopped. When you reach the intersection, wait behind the first car at the traffic light. Don't move up next to it. Drivers don't always use turn signals, so you can't be sure which way the car might turn when the light turns green.

These traffic-jam tactics are reasonably safe. But in some states or cities, it's not legal for a cyclist to pass on the right or to ride between lanes of traffic. On the other hand, it's usually legal for you (or any vehicle operator) to cautiously disobey traffic rules when the road is "obstructed."

Sidewalks and bicycle paths. Many people assume that sidewalks are safe to ride on because they put some distance between cyclists and cars. Unfortunately, sidewalks aren't safe. Stay off them unless you have no choice.

Trees, hedges, parked cars, buildings, and doorways create blind spots along a sidewalk, which is too narrow to allow you to swerve out of the way if someone crosses your path. A pedestrian can sidestep suddenly, or a small child can run out from behind an adult. Never pass a pedestrian until you have his attention.

And cars do use sidewalks—at every driveway and, in effect, at every intersection's crosswalks. You must ride very slowly and look in all directions before crossing anyplace a car may appear.

Bike paths can have these same problems. Even if bicycles are supposed to have the right of way, the path may be too narrow for safe maneuvering. Pedestrians are unpredictable, and intersections are often hazardous. A bike path can get crowded with skaters, joggers, dog walkers, and careless, inexperienced riders.

Remember, you don't have to use a bike path just because it's there. It may provide a useful shortcut, and it may be pleasant and scenic, but most bike paths are no place for competent cyclists to train or commute. Realize, though, that if you ride on a road that has a parallel bike path, some drivers may become upset. Some drivers believe that you should use a bike path if it's available. As they rush by, there is no way you can explain that the path is narrow and hazardous. Avoid this problem by choosing a different route.

Large vehicles. From your bike you can see over most cars. But don't let this vantage point lull you into a false sense of security. You can't see over a large van, a truck, or a bus. Moving blind spots lurk behind these tall vehicles.

Suppose that you are riding on a two-way, four-lane street. You have merged to the inside lane because you want to turn left. You signal and continue to move forward. You see only one other vehicle on the street: a van, coming toward you in the opposite passing lane. It stops to let you turn left. Can you safely make your turn?

No. Because you are moving forward, a blind spot behind the van is, in effect, moving toward you. If a car is passing the van in the outside lane, you won't see it. If you turn, you could have a terrible accident.

Rude drivers. Some drivers will cut in front of you. They will inch into your path from driveways and stop signs and treat you as if you had no right to the road. These people seem more dangerous than they actually are. Most are only trying to bluff you. They roll forward with one foot on the gas pedal and the other on the brake pedal, waiting to see whether you will stop.

Giving in to this bullying will slow you down and leave your self-esteem in shambles. Stand up for your rights. Don't let rude drivers spoil your ride. Outbluff them.

With a little experience—and after reading the braking tips in chapter 6—you'll have a good idea of your bike's stopping distance in any situation. You outbluff a driver by making it clear that you don't intend to stop. Continue to move forward with your pedals turning, a clear signal to the driver. Meanwhile, decide when you will have to hit the brakes in case he pulls out anyway. In most cases he won't. After all, you have the right of way, and you are behaving as though that's not open to question.

The real dangers at intersections are drivers who run stop signs or red lights without slowing down or who stop and start up again without looking. But these drivers are rare. Accidents tend to deplete their numbers.

RESPONSIBILITY BREEDS RESPECT

Cyclists annoy motorists by making the unpredictable moves that these chapters warn against. Fearful instruction—"keep away from traffic"—is passed down to children by parents who don't know much about cycling. From about 1930 to 1965, few adults in the United States rode bikes. And that was long enough for incorrect ideas about cycling to take root.

There will always be people in cars who yell, "Get off the road!" Don't let them bother you. Ride in ways that encourage drivers to maneuver around you correctly. Signal clearly. Be a good representative of cycling and a positive role model for riders in your community. When more cyclists do it right, drivers will have an easier time and become friendlier.

In the long run drivers will understand that it makes sense to share the road. Bicycles take up less space than cars, and every person who chooses to ride a bike is reducing traffic congestion and air pollution. Every day, by your presence on the road, you are helping to establish the benefits of cycling.

Riding Stronger and Longer

Your Body's Basic Energy Sources

PEDAL POWER

By Robert M. Otto, Ph.D.

Your legs gradually awaken to the movement of another ride. The early moments of this 25-miler are difficult. But after only a few minutes, your breathing increases in depth, and you begin feeling fast and efficient—like a well-tuned cycling machine. Your body is deriving energy from the most abundant source, the air itself. You feel as though you could ride forever. But how far and how fast can you actually go?

There are three energy systems that you rely on as a cyclist. By understanding these systems, you can train in ways that make energy more abundant and reliable. What follows will help you use the rest of the training information in this book.

FUEL TO BURN

The process of using energy begins with adenosine triphosphate (ATP), a compound that scientists call the currency for energy exchange in the body. Muscles can't contract without it. In fact, most life-sustaining functions depend on it.

ATP consists of an adenosine molecule linked to three phosphate molecules by high-energy chemical bonds. To liberate energy for muscular contraction, one of the phosphate molecules is released. You may not realize it as you ride, but this process is crucial. Your body's ability to satiate your muscles' need for ATP determines your performance.

Working muscles can get ATP from any of three sources, depending on the situation. When you attack a hill, you need energy released quickly. A long, flat stretch, however, calls for steady production of ATP lasting many minutes or hours. Your body senses the difference and taps the appropriate source.

ATP-PC system. A limited amount of ATP exists in the muscle cell. It's found close to a moderately high energy compound called phosphocreatine (PC). This naturally occurring and immediately available ATP source is known as the ATP-PC (adenosine triphosphate–phosphocreatine) system. It's anaerobic, which means that it doesn't need oxygen to function. And though it's the most powerful energy supply in the body, it can be exhausted by 5 to 7 seconds of intense cycling.

When this happens, the phosphocreatine splits into phosphate and creatine, creating fragments that can re-form into ATP. This extends the system's usefulness, but it still can't provide energy for more than 30 seconds. When you need a short burst of speed, this is the energy you tap. After it's depleted, it's eventually replenished by ATP from the other energy sources.

Lactic acid system. This system—also known as glycolysis—isn't as powerful as the ATP-PC system, but it lasts slightly longer. When you are on a climb or an extended sprint, this is the energy source your body draws from.

Glycolysis uses muscle glycogen (carbohydrate), then blood glucose, then finally, liver glycogen as fuel to produce energy. These substances are broken down into ATP and lactic acid. This happens within the cell but not directly at the muscle contraction site.

Because this process requires more than 10 chemical reactions, its rate of ATP production is slower than the ATP-PC system's. For up to 5 minutes, a large number of ATP molecules can be formed. But ultimately, excessive accumulation of lactic acid undermines this system by inhibiting muscular contraction. The burning sensation in your quadriceps as you attack a steep hill is an example of the accumulation of lactic acid. Fortunately, you can train your body to delay the negative effects of lactic acid buildup through repeated hard efforts, such as interval training.

Aerobic system. Of the three systems, only this one can provide energy almost indefinitely. Like the lactic acid system, it uses muscle glycogen, then blood glucose, then liver glycogen as fuel. It also taps slow-processing fat as an energy source.

What sets the aerobic system apart from the other systems is that it requires oxygen to produce ATP molecules. It also relies on more than 20 chemical reactions and a shuttle to move ATP from specialized production sites (called mitochondria) within the muscle cell to the contraction area. For these reasons the aerobic system is a slower producer of ATP, but it can produce the largest amount.

Intimately linked to the cardiorespiratory system, the aerobic system depends on a constant supply of oxygen molecules. They are inhaled into the lungs for transfer to the blood and then delivered to the muscles by the heart. Training can improve delivery by enhancing the amount of blood pumped with each heartbeat as well as the ability of muscles to extract the oxygen when it arrives.

Generally, any effort longer than 5 minutes derives the majority of its energy from the aerobic system. A prolonged ride puts a cyclist in a so-called steady state, which means that the oxygen consumed for ATP production is equal to the ATP necessary for muscle contraction. Your ability to maintain a steady state depends on a combination of your genetic potential and your fitness.

The example that began this chapter is a description of the transition between anaerobic and steady-state cycling that occurs early in a ride. Until a steady state is reached, the two anaerobic systems supply most of the ATP. So by starting out slowly you can avoid unnecessarily reducing ATP-PC or accumulating too much lactic acid. The more you train, the faster you can achieve the steady state. In just 2 minutes of riding, your aerobic system can become the predominant supplier of ATP.

CROSSING THE THRESHOLD

When you do intervals, alternating hard efforts with easy ones, your breathing becomes labored, desperate, and finally uncontrollable. Your muscles ache, and you struggle home, riding with less intensity than at any time during the day. You're spent.

Any extreme effort, such as a long sprint or climb, bathes muscles with lactic acid. Given time to recover, such as on a descent, the muscles partially clear themselves until the next hard burst. But they are never totally cleared on a given ride. The accumulation eventually allows lactic acid to cause fatigue and breathlessness.

At this point you can no longer rely on your first energy source. Phosphocreatine, having completed its short-term mission, is depleted. Your second energy source is paralyzed by its own by-product, lactic acid. So your body is forced to use only oxygen to produce ATP, and the aerobic system can't provide energy as fast as your muscles need it.

The point at which lactic acid becomes debilitating is called the anaerobic threshold (AT). For competitive cyclists, race pace is just below AT, which allows them to use both aerobic and anaerobic energy. AT is one of the best indicators of endurance performance. For the untrained it usually occurs at 65 to 75 percent of max VO_2. (Max VO_2, or maximum oxygen uptake, is a prime predictor of your ability as an endurance athlete. It is a laboratory measurement of how much oxygen you can breathe in and process in 1 minute. This test can be taken at sports-medicine clinics or universities. If you don't know your max VO_2, base your workout efforts on heart rate, as explained in the next chapter.) A well-trained cyclist may raise his or her heart rate to more than 85 percent of max VO_2.

ENERGY ENHANCERS

Here are four ways to increase the performance of your energy systems.

Go the distance. Your max VO_2 is largely determined by genetics, so improving it isn't easy. Your best bet is to ride just below your AT for as long as you can. Begin by trying to maintain this intensity for 10 to 30 minutes. As your endurance increases, lengthen your workouts accordingly. This type of high-intensity endurance work may raise your max VO_2.

Ride hard, rest easy. Use interval training to increase your AT. This prevents lactic acid accumulation from disrupting high-intensity efforts. In fact, such training can increase the amount of creatine, phosphate, and ATP in your system and enhance the use of some of the lactic acid.

Using your heart rate as a guide, ride for 10 to 20 seconds at a pace that produces a pulse equal to 80 to 90 percent of that reached at your max VO_2, then follow with a lower-intensity period of 1 to 3 minutes. As your AT rises, lengthen the work interval and shorten the recovery period. Be sure that you give yourself an easy day after such intense training.

Build tolerance. Train with hill repeats and other hard efforts to teach your body to withstand increased amounts of lactic acid. This allows you to continue riding above your AT for longer periods, which is important for climbing and sprinting.

There are two excellent methods for increasing lactic acid tolerance. The first is to do intervals lasting from 20 seconds to 3 minutes, interspersed with 30 to 60 seconds of recovery. Keep the recovery interval short to make sure that the lactic acid level in your muscles stays high. The second method is to do a long 20- to 60-minute workout at AT intensity with no recovery period.

Show your muscle. Use weight training and sprinting to increase the size of your quadriceps and other muscle groups involved in pedaling. For endurance efforts, which are spent mostly in steady state, you don't need the extra bulk. But to become a better sprinter and improve your power, increasing your muscle size results in a greater quantity of readily available ATP-PC.

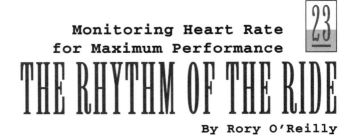

THE RHYTHM OF THE RIDE

By Rory O'Reilly

For many people, simply riding at a heart rate greater than about 130 beats per minute will ensure an aerobic benefit. But for performance-minded cyclists, the best place to start is with a maximum heart-rate test. It's hard but worthwhile, because the common formula of "220 minus your age" is notoriously inaccurate. If your pulse is naturally high, then the standard training range recommendations will be too easy. The opposite also applies.

You should be in good condition before taking the test, or your legs or lungs will tire before you have achieved your true maximum heart rate. Make sure that you get your doctor's approval.

It's possible to do the test on the road. You may even attain your max at the top of a hill during a hard group ride. But indoors on a stationary trainer is a better, more-controlled environment.

You will need a friend to assist. The goal is to reach your max in about 15 minutes. Shift onto the large chainring and one of the larger rear cogs. Start pedaling and achieve a heart rate of 120 to 130 beats per minute, an easy pace for most riders. Throughout the test you must maintain a cadence of 80 to 90 revolutions per minute. Use a metronome, or a cycle computer with a cadence function, or have your friend count pedal strokes for 15 seconds each minute and multiply by four.

Using a heart-rate monitor, have your friend record your heart rate every minute, too. An appropriate increase is two or three beats per minute. Usually shifting to the next smaller cog works perfectly. If you can't get enough resistance on your trainer by using its settings, reduce the tire pressure and move the roller harder against the tread.

AND THE BEAT GOES ON

The days of taking your pulse with your fingers on your wrist are quickly fading away. Thanks to heart-rate monitors, you can receive immediate feedback on how fast your heart is beating. The monitor consists of two parts: a transmission belt strapped around the chest that relays the heart-rate signal wirelessly to a receiver (on a watch or a handlebar). The receiver continuously displays the heart rate in beats per minute.

Monitors are lightweight, waterproof, and available in most bike shops and sporting goods stores. Their price ranges from $80 to $400, depending on the features you want, such as memory, limit alarms, and download capability.

As you approach your max, your friend should shout lots of encouragement to continue. Remember, this is a maximal test. It's hard work. It's going to hurt. You must push yourself until you absolutely cannot maintain an 80-plus cadence. At this point, the number on your heart-rate monitor is your maximum heart rate.

MAKE THE MOST OF YOUR MAX

As a coach, I have my riders do very little anaerobic threshold (AT) work at the start of the season. Your AT is the point at which your muscle efficiency falls off significantly. High-intensity cycling is stressful, and you need to gradually build to it. Conversely, I try to keep them from training below the basic endurance level (the point where the heart rate is high enough to develop aerobic fitness) because it has no benefit. In fact, I call anything below 125 beats per minute garbage training because it won't contribute to improvement. If you have ever wondered how someone who rides fewer than 200 miles a week can beat someone who does more than 400, chances are that the latter does too much garbage.

Keep in mind that you will always spend time below the basic endurance level, such as when warming up or cooling down. And it's impossible to keep your pulse elevated on long descents.

Starting in March, my team's training is divided into time segments this way: 10 percent in zone 4, 25 to 30 percent in zone 3, and 60 to 65 percent in zone 2. (Refer to "Training in the Zone.") This may not sound hard, but it takes discipline and concentration.

PROGRAM YOUR TRAINING

Divide rides into minutes spent in each of the zones and record this information in a training diary. With a basic heart-rate monitor you will need to estimate. Deluxe models can tell you how much time you spend below, within, and above a preprogrammed range. The best option, and the one I use with my riders, involves the Polar computer interface. Cabled to a personal computer, it can quickly divide rides into time spent in specific zones, then produce graphs. This is invaluable when working with a team.

For my riders, Saturday, Sunday, Wednesday, and Thursday are hard days. These can involve structured intervals or simply fast group rides.

I prefer doing intervals on a marked 1-kilometer section of road. After a warmup, the riders complete the section in zone 4 (AT range), then pedal easily in zone 2 (easy aerobic range) back to the start. They repeat this sequence four to 10 times. One-kilometer hill repeats are also effective. Recovery occurs when coasting downhill.

Granted, this is an intense program designed for racers, but it illustrates a heart-rate monitor's usefulness and how it is incorporated into training. Use the same tenets to organize a program that's right for you.

TRAINING IN THE ZONE

After you determine your maximum heart rate, calculate your intensity zones. Knowing these numbers can ensure that you maintain a heart rate that delivers the most benefit for what you want to accomplish on each ride.

Zone	Max Heart Rate (%)	Benefits
1	65	Recovery
2	66–72	Basic endurance and aerobic capacity
3	73–79	Higher-level aerobic capacity
4	85–90	Anaerobic threshold work and improved time trials
5	91–100	Sprints and anaerobic power

Note: No cycling is called for in the 80 to 84 percent range. This is considered "no man's land"—too high for the steady tempo of zone 3 and not hard enough to stimulate the improvement of zone 4.

For instance, you may do intervals on Tuesday and Thursday, go easy on Wednesday and Friday, work on endurance on Saturday, do a fast group ride on Sunday, then take Monday off.

It's important to monitor easy days as well as hard ones. Without rest you won't be able to train hard enough, recover, and grow stronger. A monitor also helps you avoid overtraining. Signs of overtraining include an elevated pulse during easy rides and warmups and poor recovery between intervals. Another sign that many cyclists don't recognize is the inability to achieve a high heart rate even though they are riding extremely hard and their legs have a lactic acid burn.

Interval Training
for Endurance and Speed

TAKE IT TO THE LIMIT

By Geoff Drake

David Farmer, a physical therapist and personal coach to several world-class bike racers, knows how reality can pull a U-turn on science. In a race or another important event, laboratory predictions of heart rate can have all the reliability of a Ouija board. He has seen riders burst through barriers that seemed impenetrable on paper, leaving a trail of formulas in their wake.

"A book may tell you that you can hold an ergometer test for so many minutes, but a race will tell you otherwise," Farmer says. "I'll often prescribe intervals at a higher training heart rate, based on what my riders have shown me they can do in a race. You have to take adrenaline into account."

Recommendations for heart-rate levels are as different as the coaches who prescribe them. For instance, in his *Complete Book of Bicycling*, Greg LeMond recommends that a "light-intensity" workout be done at a tongue-dragging 80 to 90 percent of maximum heart rate. Others call this same level time-trial pace. Still others prescribe a training heart rate that corresponds to maximum oxygen update.

SETTING YOUR PACE

Everything starts with determining your maximum heart rate. You can use the method described in chapter 23. Or you can do it on the road, noting your heart rate at the top of a long, steep, all-out climb.

This maximum figure supplies a training reference point. Keep in mind, however, that it isn't a measure of performance. Your max is genetically determined and won't change much from year to year (though it will gradually decline as you age). What will change is the

INTERVALS MADE EASY

Intervals can be onerous. They hurt, so any enthusiasm that you initially have won't last long, even though you see improvement. For this reason I recommend "recreational" intervals, which will make you better without making you bitter.

As opposed to traditional intervals, the recreational variety has less structure and pressure. With this workout, you simply include several bursts to sustained top speed during the course of one or two rides each week. These are done when the spirit moves you, and the period between each "on" effort can be as long or as short as you like. These won't be quite as effective as structured intervals, but you are more likely to continue doing them.

All it takes is to jump hard out of the saddle, wind up your gear, sit down, and pedal hard for a minute or more. You can create challenges for motivation: Tell yourself to keep going to that road sign or that silo in the distance. Then roll easy until you feel like stretching yourself again. It may happen in 2 minutes or 15 minutes. It doesn't make any difference, as long as you are surging past your anaerobic threshold several times during the ride.

That said, some riders prefer (or need) the gun-to-the-head motivation of structured intervals. When the schedule says go, you go. When it says stop, you stop. If you want to try it this way, here is an effective workout.

percentage of max that you can maintain. In fact, Farmer says that this phrase should be written large in your training diary: "Focus on working at a higher percentage of max." More than any other type of training, intervals are what makes this possible.

The traditional next step is to do some grade-school multiplication to determine training intensity zones. But, just as with using a formula to calculate maximum heart rate, here's another place you need to be careful. Many riders find that the level they can maintain in a race far exceeds the anaerobic threshold (AT) level derived from a formula.

For this reason Farmer cautions against a cookbook approach for racers. "A rider might determine that his AT is 157 with a formula, but in a race he can maintain 167 for 2 hours," he says. His tests of elite riders have shown AT levels from 80 to 93 percent of max. This is based on what he calls a functional definition, or "the level that you can maintain for the length of the race you want to do." Typically, this in-

1. Warm up for at least 15 minutes by spinning in a moderate gear, such as a 39 × 17-tooth (39 × 17T) gear. Increase your gear and pace in the last few minutes.

2. Choose a fairly large gear (say, 53 × 17T) that you can turn at 90 to 100 revolutions per minute for the duration of each "on" interval. Stand and sprint to get the gear turning, then sit and push hard for 90 seconds. During the last 20 to 30 seconds, your heart rate should reach 90 percent of maximum.

3. Shift back to your moderate gear and spin easy until your heart rate falls to 60 percent of max.

4. Immediately shift up and go again, but this time let off after 75 seconds. This shorter work interval allows you to maintain full effort for the duration, despite fatigue from the first effort.

5. Repeat step 3.

6. Continue to alternate big-gear hard riding with moderate-gear easy spinning. Decrease each "on" interval by 15 seconds until you are down to 30 seconds. Then you're done.

7. Cool down with 20 minutes of easy spinning on your way home.

—Fred Matheny

formation is gathered via a heart-rate monitor with a memory feature, such as the Polar Vantage XL. Results can then be graphed using Polar's computer interface.

GETTING UP TO SPEED

The important thing is that this functional AT level should rise during the season. One Farmer disciple, the recently retired mountain biker Ned Overend, found that his AT could be as low as the 150s in March and as high as 170 when he was peaking for a major event in midsummer. "Basing it on a percentage of max has nowhere near the validity of what you know you can maintain in a race," confirms Overend.

Your interval regimen should produce an increase like Overend experienced. For example, you may start the season able to do five 3-minute intervals at 155 beats per minute. With effective training you could complete the same set at perhaps 165 beats per minute. Congratulations—you have raised your AT. Now you can ride longer at a higher heart rate, which means that you are faster. Conversely, if you can't achieve the same level that you could earlier in the season, consider it a sign of overtraining.

Interval workouts should vary according to your goals. Longer "on" phases (3 to 10 minutes) are best for steady-state events, such as time trials and century rides. Emphasize shorter intervals (30 seconds to 3 minutes) for events that require repeated quick bursts, such as criteriums.

In either case allow only partial recovery between each "on" phase. For most of us interval workouts should be limited to two per week (and never on consecutive days). Otherwise, there is a risk of excessive intensity and overtraining.

Go Fast to Go Far

LONG-DISTANCE SECRETS

By Ed Pavelka

Pete Penseyres is a grandfather in his fifties, but he's still winning bike races, including national masters championships. That's a credit to his fitness, talent, and racing savvy. But as a spry 43-year-old back in 1986, he did something that becomes even more remarkable with each passing season. That's the year he won the Race Across America (RAAM) with an average speed of 15.4 miles per hour, a performance still hailed as "the greatest in RAAM history." His transcontinental time of 8 days, 9 hours, 47 minutes has been bettered as shorter routes have been used, but no one has ever ridden across the United States at a faster pace.

That's one reason it pays to listen to Penseyres. For, you see, what he accomplished in 1986 is much more than mere history. It introduced a key new concept to endurance training that still isn't understood or applied by many riders. We're talking about speedwork, training that makes it as easy to ride long distances at 18 miles per hour, for instance, as at 16 miles per hour. Best of all, it's as applicable to recreational century riders as it is to RAAM racers.

In the following interview Penseyres explains how he discovered the benefits of speedwork and the results it brought him. He won the 1984 RAAM in a record 9 days, 13 hours using conventional long-distance training (miles, miles, and more miles), then sat out 1985 to help his brother Jim, a Vietnam veteran and amputee, achieve his dream of riding the race. That's the same year Jonathan Boyer, the first American to compete in the Tour de France, decided to show everyone what a "real racer" could do in RAAM. And he did, not only winning but taking a half-day off Penseyres's 1984 record.

This didn't sit well with Penseyres. Although a road racer, too, he was a leader of the ultramarathon "family" and took offense at Boyer's criticisms of the RAAM riders' techniques and talents. Boyer was expected to enter RAAM again in 1986, and Penseyres figured the best way to answer him was to go head-to-head with him.

Just weeks before the start, however, Boyer decided not to race. In an act of RAAM legend, Penseyres's wife and crew chief, Joanne, intercepted the press release and kept the news from him so that it wouldn't ruin his motivation. But Penseyres still had Boyer's record to beat. With this impetus and a strong challenge from another talented rider, Michael Secrest, Penseyres crushed Boyer's mark with a pace that has never been equaled.

Something besides revenge and desire was at work, though. Penseyres also needed speed. Here he tells how he got it—and how you can become a better long-distance cyclist by training fast instead of just long.

Q. How did you discover that training faster is essential for improving long-distance performance?

A. It just evolved as I changed my training program prior to each RAAM. There was no book on ultramarathon racing then, so we all just started trying things that we thought would work best. When I first rode RAAM in 1983, my thinking was that all you need to do is ride a lot of miles. Long, steady distance training would be plenty. So I was riding back and forth to work and doing extra distance in the morning and evening. My regular one-way commute was 30 miles, and I was adding 10 miles on my way in, then riding 60 to 70 miles on the way home. I was getting in 110 miles a day, and on weekends I would do a double century on Saturday and again on Sunday. So I was doing 1,000 to 1,100 miles a week. This was for the month before the race.

Q. That's a heavy load! What kind of shape did it leave you in at work?

A. It was a desk job at a nuclear generating station in San Clemente, California. So, actually, work was the recovery phase for the double workout. That's one of the beauties of being able to commute and train at the same time—especially at a place that has showers. You jump in, you feel good, you get clean, and you're ready for work. You forget about cycling for 8 hours and focus on other things. When you get off work, you have to get home anyhow, so it's just automatic to ride again. This makes it a lot easier mentally.

Q. What did you do to improve your second-place finish in 1983 to first place in 1984?

A. Instead of doing the double centuries on the weekends, I thought that it would make a lot more sense to do what you do in RAAM at least one day a week, which is ride for 24 hours. So I'd start right after work on Friday night and ride until Saturday night. The thing I liked about it is that I could take Sunday off. I'd sleep from Saturday night until whenever.

Q. Still no speed?

A. No. I never focused on speed. When I was commuting home, my average speed was 15 to 16 miles per hour, sometimes 17. I avoided racing—both local training races and USCF (United States Cycling Federation) events—because I was afraid of crashing and having an injury that would keep me out of RAAM. Maybe I did a couple of races early in the season, but it wasn't part of my training regimen.

Q. What changed your mind?

A. After Boyer won RAAM in 1985, and I thought that he was going to come back in 1986, I knew that the only way I could beat him was to be as fast as he was. So I threw out the book and said, okay, I have to do some speedwork. I'm not going to worry about the miles. It's still necessary to do one long ride on the weekends—in my case, a 400-miler. I'm still convinced that's a real good thing. Even if it doesn't work for endurance—which I think that it does, because it builds your mental toughness so that you know you can go for 24 hours—it certainly helps you find little problems that won't show up on shorter rides. You may discover that your shorts are bugging you or that there's something wrong with your position on the bike and you start to have knee trouble. I could find these things on a 400-mile ride a lot easier than on a 100-mile ride, just like many riders will learn more on a 75-miler than on a 25-miler.

Q. How did you add the speedwork?

A. I started focusing on training races. There was a convenient race that took place on Tuesday and Thursday evenings, going right past the power plant. I just stayed late after work and rode with that group. It was a 35-mile race, with 20 to 30 people. It was really fast and competitive, and I made it even tougher by using my commute bike. It weighed about 35 pounds, with fenders, lights, and batteries. And the other riders worked me over on purpose to get me ready, because they knew what I was doing. You know, "Let's get Pete ready to beat Boyer in RAAM." They trashed me twice a week.

I also rode a team time trial on Monday, Wednesday, and Friday mornings. The time trial was only 6½ miles, but we went as hard as we could. Teams had from two to four riders, depending on how many showed up. It was flat, down and back, and we timed it, so we got a good feel for our conditioning. The usual time was around 15 minutes. It was more like structured intervals than anything else I did, because I got a chance to rest a bit in the paceline. We did these in the morning before work. I'd commute in, and we'd go.

Q. Hold it. You've gone from no speedwork to five consecutive days of speedwork. Isn't that too much intense training?

A. Proportionally, the intense stuff was not a whole lot of mileage, although it was as intense as I could make it. I was doing about 20 miles of all-out team time trialing and about 70 miles of road racing each week. So only about a tenth of my weekly mileage was at this level.

What it did was reduce the time it took for my 400-mile rides by about 3 hours, and I was about 10 minutes faster on each leg of my commute. It had the intended effect—it raised my cruising speed by about 10 percent, or by at least 1 mile per hour. For the same perceived effort, or the same heart rate, I was going faster. My anaerobic threshold was higher, so I was comfortable at a faster speed.

Q. And that's the benefit missed by riding long, steady distance all the time?

A. Right. Your training should be geared to elevating your steady pace. You're trying to increase your efficiency, whether it's measured in calories burned per mile or heart rate. Speedwork makes a big difference in moving up the anaerobic threshold. Then you become more efficient—you're faster for the same effort.

Q. Most people would say that there can't be a relationship between training for RAAM and training for a century, a double century, or another long one-day ride. Obviously, you believe that there is.

A. Speedwork is the key for RAAM, so it has to be the key for anything that's shorter than RAAM. The trouble is, it goes against logic. You know that you're not going to ride the event in a way that resembles speed training. But on the other hand, your cruising speed goes up a mile or two per hour.

People have asked me, "I've done a lot of centuries, and now I want to do the fastest one I can. How do I get faster?" You go out and do anaerobic threshold stuff. Push yourself as high as you can on heart rate, then recover and do it again. The best way to do it is in training races because you're doing it with other people and it's not something you have to force. Either you do it or you get dropped.

Q. You've mentioned training races a lot. What about going out by yourself for an interval workout?

A. Structured intervals would probably be great, but I can't force myself to do those anymore. I've been racing for 20 years. Intervals hurt too much, and I don't like to do them alone. I can't do intervals with the intensity that I need for them to do me any good. But really, hard training is basically the same, whether you're in a practice race or jamming down the road by yourself. As long as your heart is being pushed through the anaerobic threshold, it doesn't matter how.

Q. How many speed workouts would you recommend each week for a competitive long-distance rider?

A. I think that you need at least three. Going by the people I time-trialed with, the ones who came out three times a week definitely got faster. The ones who came out twice a week maintained whatever level they had. And the folks who came out only once a week got dropped. This is pretty subjective, but I think that three times a week is minimum to improve speed.

In my case the 15-minute sessions on Mondays, Wednesdays, and Fridays were the best 45 minutes I could spend on a bike. I pushed my heart rate way above the anaerobic threshold. And I did it a number of times, since this was a team time trial. Every time I got to the front I'd go anaerobic, and then I'd have to go even harder trying to get back on the end of the line. These weren't classic intervals because there wasn't much recovery sitting in. My heart rate dropped from 170 to 155 before it was time to pull again, which maybe wasn't ideal. But riding this way was so much fun compared with solo, structured intervals.

It's easy to go out and ride long, steady distance, and it's hard to force yourself to do speedwork. But riding long and steady for endurance is necessary only once a week. It's the speedwork that does the most for your century time.

Q. How else does speedwork translate to a long one-day ride?

A. A lot of times you have the opportunity to ride in a paceline. If you want to take advantage of drafting people to get your fastest time for the distance, then you have to be able to match their speeds by frequently varying yours. On the other hand, if you want to do your fastest time on your own, then you need to maintain the steadiest pace you can. Push the climbs, because that's where you can lose the most time. Then ride all the rest of it steadily.

Q. Push the climbs? Long-distance riders usually say that the key on hills is to always stay below the anaerobic threshold.

A. For a century, a double, or RAAM, if you want to do your fastest time, the best thing is to be as steady as possible. But if there's one place you won't do that, it's on climbs. My tactic is to put a little extra effort into a climb and go a couple of miles an hour faster, then coast on the descent, where the time difference between pedaling your fanny off and coasting is minimal. You spend a lot more time climbing, and the percentage difference between 10 and 12 miles per hour on a climb is a lot more than, say, the percentage difference between 35 and 37 miles per hour for the much shorter time on the descent. If you look at it from this standpoint, the only place you'd ever want to put out extra effort is on the climbs. You pay for it later—you won't be able to go quite so hard on the flats—but that's okay, because you still make time. You're still better off overall. You just don't want to get carried away to the extent that you blow up. Don't go anaerobic. But if you can climb fast, that's a big advantage for long-distance events.

Q. You're known as an outstanding climber, whether in road races or ultramarathon events. How do you train on hills?

A. My commute had plenty of hills, and I used some of them to push myself to near or above my anaerobic threshold. This may not have been as good as repeat intervals on the same hill, but it still made a huge difference in my climbing.

For instance, there was a hill on my way to work that I sometimes used as a gauge. It was long enough that I couldn't sprint—½ mile or so of 7 percent grade—and I was on a loaded bike. If I was really flying, I could hold 14 to 15 miles per hour. But in the winter, if I hadn't been doing much speedwork at all, I was lucky to hold 10 miles per hour. That's a difference of almost 50 percent with the same perceived effort, and it was totally due to speedwork and working hard on climbing. Of course, I didn't jam this hill flat out every day. I may have jammed it once a week, or only once every couple of months in winter.

Q. It's interesting how much training you were able to fit into commuting before you retired.

A. I can't imagine why more people don't do it. Commuting is really the best way to be able to race and ride long-distance events. I think that a lot more cyclists are starting to commute, including those you'd think of as only competitors. People are getting smart about the fact that it doesn't make any sense spending time in a car going to work when you can train that way.

Q. Okay. We've become a lot faster, and we've maintained our endurance. The third key to good long-distance performance is nutrition. RAAM riders are known for using liquid diets and other special foods. Are these helpful for regular riders, too?

A. Yes, you probably get a small improvement with liquid food. But for a one-day ride it's more important not to try anything that could result in an upset stomach. Besides, you store a substantial amount of your energy before the ride. For a running marathon you can store 2 to 3 hours' worth. I think that this equals 5 to 6 hours' worth in cycling. So it's okay to nibble away on bananas and other solid food and not worry about special diets.

In the 1986 RAAM it wasn't until day two that I started noticing the difference with liquid food. On day one you're still running off the stored stuff. After that is when liquid food makes a big, big difference. But for century rides, eat what you know you can tolerate. If you do decide to use a liquid diet to get that extra edge, make sure you try it in training to be certain you can digest it.

We always try to reinvent the wheel, but some of the things that people have done for years just make so much sense. You're reminded of this sometimes. A friend of mine was cruising around San Diego and ran into this neat old guy out on his classic Masi bicycle. You could tell by his riding style that he had probably raced. My friend started talking to him and found out that he had indeed competed back in the 1950s. So my friend said, "Tell me, what did you use at the end of a race to give you a little kick?" And the guy said, "Flat Coke." That's exactly what we're using in races right now. It's good to know that some things never change.

Q. One thing that does change is age. Yet when you turned 50, you celebrated by becoming a USCF national masters champion. At 53, you competed in RAAM again as a member of *Bicycling* magazine's senior team—and you helped set a record of 5 days, 11 hours. Has your training kept you as strong as ever?

A. No, not quite. There are certain rides I can look back on year after year, such as the Death Valley–Mount Whitney Road Race. Even though it's done in a pack, it breaks up on the second day and turns into a time trial. I've noticed an improvement in the past couple of years by going to a lighter bike, but overall, I can see a gradual slow-down in my time. It's a very slow trailing-off, but it's there. There's no denying it.

Q. One theory is that if you maintain a high level of fitness year after year, with no lay-offs, the decline is so gradual that it seems to not be happening.

A. I think that's right. People who stop competing and then try to come back struggle badly at first. And maybe they do come back to where they would have been otherwise, but it's awfully hard for them. I think that it's much easier to try to maintain your fitness as long as you can, especially if you want to be competitive in your age group. The best thing you can do is to keep going. It's just like the old machinist tells the young apprentice: Rust never sleeps.

Build Strength with Gravity's Help

THE UPSIDE OF HILLS

By Ed Pavelka

ere's a guarantee: If you live where you can climb on every ride, you can forget about training and still become a strong rider. Think about it. Every time you ascend a hill, you strengthen your leg muscles and boost your heart rate to the anaerobic threshold or beyond, then recover on the descent. Who needs formal interval training when you can get the same effect (and have more fun) by riding hills?

If you are looking for proof, then I'm your man. I come from hills and dales. Back in 1985, when I moved from Vermont to Pennsylvania, I found the cycling much tougher. Instead of occasional climbs, I faced endless climbs. The final indignity came at the end of every ride. A dozen roads led back toward my home, and each rises 500 vertical feet.

Initially, I dreaded all this climbing. Like all big riders, I'm gravitationally challenged. Going up had always been my downfall. But these hills made me stronger than I had been in 20 years of cycling. I got personal records in time trials from 7 to 100 miles. I averaged 140 miles per day on a transcontinental ride. I broke the New York cross-state record on a route with 12,000 vertical feet. And I did these things without even one session of traditional interval training. All I did was climb lots of hills.

I'm convinced that nothing will get you fitter and keep you fitter than climbing, if you do it regularly. Of course, not everyone is fortunate enough to live in hilly terrain. But even if you have only one decent hill in your area, that's enough. You can still get climbing's benefits by doing hill intervals. You'll have to work at it—you can't amass vertical feet in normal riding—but the rewards can be nearly as great.

RIDING HIGH

The ideal hill for intervals is about ¾ mile long. This training is simple (at least to describe). After warming up well, you ride hard to the top of the hill, coast down to recover, then go again. You may need to do a few loops at the bottom of the hill until your heart rate falls to 60 percent of maximum, which means you have recovered sufficiently.

The basic hill workout includes gear changes to increase pedaling resistance and improve technique. Here's an example: The first time up, use a gear that you can turn fairly easily from the saddle—say, 39 × 23-tooth (39 × 23T). The next time, start in the 21T cog. A bit tougher, eh? Then when you get about 200 yards from the top, shift to the 19T cog, stand, and sprint. You'll be blown, but after recovery you may be able to repeat this one or more times. Do what you can without falling apart.

If the hill is longer, don't initially go all the way to the top. Build your strength with consistent weekly workouts. You'll be able to handle the whole hill before long. It's also useful to vary your workouts by riding harder than usual to points below the top, then turning back to recover. If the hill is quite short or not very steep, compensate by using bigger gears or more repeats, or do the workout on days when there is also a headwind.

Work on your climbing technique during this training. (See chapter 8 for pointers.) Do not make the common mistake of shifting to lower gears as a hill wears on. When riding with others, use the lowest gear that lets you keep up with them as the hill starts. Then your legs will be fresh enough to shift to higher gears in the last half, gaining speed instead of losing it. This concept was new to American riders until Poland's Eddie Borysewicz was hired to coach the national team. "Climbing," says Borysewicz, "is a matter of increasing the gear size, never decreasing it. When you go to a lower gear, you slow down, and then you get dropped."

Climbing intervals also help develop your out-of-saddle riding technique. Immediately before standing, shift to the next smaller cog (higher gear) so that you maintain speed. This is necessary because pedal revolutions per minute decrease when you leave the saddle. Use your body weight to help push the pedals down, but be careful not to let the bike waver on the road. It should maintain a straight line while your body moves over it. This takes upper-body strength plus the coordination that comes only with practice.

FAKING IT

Most cyclists say that they hate two things: hills and headwinds. Well, if you don't have any climbs on which to train, you had better learn to love stiff breezes. Headwinds are the only reasonable substitute for climbing.

Fake a hill by pedaling a big gear directly into the wind. The correct gear allows a cadence of 80 to 90 revolutions per minute, with a heart rate that nudges past your anaerobic threshold by the end—just like at the top of a climb. Do this training like hill intervals, turning back after several minutes to recover with the tailwind. The results won't be as impressive as those you would get from hill work, but your power will improve.

RIDE LIKE THE WIND

By Davis Phinney

Serious attention to aerodynamics is relatively new in cycling. It wasn't until the late 1980s, for instance, that aero handlebars appeared in the Tour de France. But what an impression they made. Greg LeMond used an aero bar in the final stage of the 1989 Tour—a time trial—to overcome a 50-second deficit and win the overall title by 8 seconds, the closest finish in Tour history. No one failed to notice that the rider who LeMond caught and passed that day, France's Laurent Fignon, was not using aero equipment. Cyclists have been getting more sleek and slippery ever since.

Wind tunnel tests show that a significant drag reduction is possible with relatively minor changes in position and equipment. Lower drag means you can trim your time without increasing effort. And it doesn't matter whether your goal is the local time trial, a faster century, or just the feeling of slicing the wind on your daily ride.

Fortunately, you don't need exotic equipment or wind tunnel testing to benefit from aerodynamics. Just try these three simple tricks.

SIT SMALL

Let's assume that you are situated correctly on your bike: Your seat is adjusted to the proper height, your pelvis is tipped forward, and your back is flat. If so, don't make wholesale changes. You are most efficient in your accustomed position. So how can you get more aero without sapping that hard-won pedaling efficiency?

Simple. Streamline your body by narrowing your arms and shoulders and lowering your upper body (bend those elbows). And bring

POSTURE MAKES PERFECT

How does Chris Boardman do it?

In 1996, the Englishman set a world record by riding 34.8 miles in 1 hour, establishing himself as the premier time trialist in pro cycling. He couldn't have accomplished this without having an aerodynamic position that's second to none.

Boardman, like most top time trialists, can sustain a radical aero position for several reasons. First, his time trial bike has a seat-tube angle that's steeper than your road bike's—at least 78 degrees versus 73 degrees. This moves his saddle forward, which means he can get low but still open the angle formed by his femur and upper body at the top of the pedal stroke. His thighs don't hit his chest, so his breathing isn't compromised.

To get the same benefit, you don't need to buy a new bike designed for time trialing. Several companies manufacture angled seatposts, aimed at triathletes, that move the saddle forward like a frame with a steep seat tube. Ask at your bike shop.

Second, good time trialists are flexible in their hamstrings and lower backs. Cycling trainer Andrew Pruitt, Ed.D., director of Table Mesa Sports and Rehabilitation in Boulder, Colorado, argues that if you can't touch your toes when your knees are straight and without a warmup, you will have trouble achieving an aero position. Dr. Pruitt, in his role as chief medical officer for the U.S. Cycling Federation, has worked with Lance

your knees closer to the top tube while pedaling to minimize your profile. Thinking low and narrow is the first step to aero efficiency.

GET A BETTER GRIP

My time trial position is exactly like my road setup, with one simple addition—a set of aero bars that are easily bolted to a standard drop handlebar. Aero bars are a quick and inexpensive way for any rider to get a measurable benefit. In fact, studies show that they can potentially knock more than 2 minutes off your 40-K (25-mile) time trial.

Aero bars allow you to rest your forearms in cupped pads, with your hands gripping the extensions for control and leverage. The bars bring your elbows and shoulders down and together. In order to get flatter and more comfortable, some riders push their saddles forward, but this is unnecessary if your basic position is good.

A word of caution: It takes a ride or two to get used to aero bars.

Armstrong on his time trialing position. Some of Armstrong's improvement in this discipline can be traced to greater flexibility.

For exercises to improve your flexibility, check out the book *Stretching*, by Bob Anderson. But if you are naturally tight, you may have to forgo an extremely low position.

Finally, find a balance between the position that produces maximum aerodynamic benefits and the position that enables you to generate maximum power. They are rarely the same. The best way to find your optimum aero position is to do coast-down testing.

On a long hill with a steady grade, time yourself coasting down in various positions. Then check your power output by riding your bike on a stationary trainer, using progressively larger gears and comparing them with your heart rate. The bigger the gear that you can use for a given heart rate, the greater your power. Once you know where you are most aero and where you are most powerful, find a middle ground that translates to the greatest speed on the road.

Don't worry if you can't get as low and stretched out as Boardman. Some other top time trialists, such as five-time Tour de France winner Miguel Indurain, sit fairly high on their bikes. This occurs because the power from their standard road positions overrides the wind-cheating advantages of a lower but less-efficient position.

—Fred Matheny

Your bike handles differently when your weight is on them. And because your hands are far from the brake levers, don't use aero bars in a group or on descents. Although my competitive days are over, I still like aero bars because I find the position comfortable on long rides.

Some alternatives to conventional aero bars include Scott Rakes, Cinelli Spinaci, and 3T Tirumisu. These products bolt to a drop bar to let you assume an aero position for short periods. They are light and uncomplicated, but they don't have armrests for comfort. Rakes mount next to the stem, like a narrow pair of drops. The Cinelli and 3T products resemble the bar-ends found on mountain bikes, but they are attached in board on the handlebar top, curving in front of the stem. You can get low and narrow on them, but because your forearms rest on the handlebar, long-distance comfort is lacking. All these products are handy when you are riding against a headwind, leading a paceline, or needing extra speed for any reason.

Chris Boardman shows the position and equipment that made him pro cycling's top time trialist.

RIDE A GOOD SET OF WHEELS

Until recently, technology was quite limited for road wheels. Conventionally spoked wheels were slow because they created drag with their turbulence—the so-called egg-beater effect. Composite wheels were sleeker but often rode harshly.

One new solution is Spinergy's Rev-X composite wheels. These have only four pairs of thin composite spokes, so turbulence is reduced. I have ridden these wheels for a couple of years and appreciate their durability and forgiving ride—more like spoked wheels rather than composites.

Many other manufacturers make aero wheels, including Specialized, Zipp, Campagnolo, HED, and Mavic. These wheels can improve your bike's appearance as well as its performance.

There is one downside, though. Because their deep, V-shaped rims present a broad side surface, aero wheels can cause handling problems in strong crosswinds. They also react differently in corners, so take it easy at first. And because they aren't cheap (usually $350 to $450 per wheel), make sure to check their replacement policy before you buy.

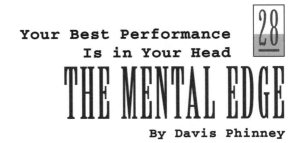

Your Best Performance
Is in Your Head

THE MENTAL EDGE

By Davis Phinney

To be successful you need to set goals. Whether you are gearing up for a big ride or race or you just want to get over the next hill, goals are important. And perhaps more than anything, it's your ability to focus that helps you reach your goals.

Focus can be described as narrowing your attention. Focus is concentration. It lets you aim your vision and define your view. You choose a goal (a major event such as a tour, a bike camp, or a race you want to be in shape for) and commit to preparing for it. Staying focused on the goal—sustaining a strong mental image of the event—makes it easier for you to put in the necessary work. You will get out the door for rides that you may otherwise be tempted to skip.

Like the focusing power of a camera, mental focus lets you see things more clearly and concentrate on what's important. But unlike modern cameras, autofocus in your mind is not an option. You must develop the skill to zero in on the right elements. Concentrating on the long-term goal is good, but don't forget about the short-term goals that get you there.

Here's an example. Before the 1984 Olympics in Los Angeles, I focused so much on this long-term goal that I lost the ability to enjoy riding in the short term. For almost two years before the Games, I was obsessed with that event, especially the road race. I created an image of the day in my mind so often that I was unable to think about much else.

I was adrift in a sea of Olympic hype, so much so that I didn't appreciate the remarkable races and improvements that occurred during that time. My expectation was so high—winning was my only objective—that I set myself up for failure. I lost, finishing fifth in the road race and third in the team time trial.

Through that experience I realized that the steps up the ladder should be savored and valued. Proper focus is putting blinders on, but not so tightly that you miss what's right in front of you. Visualizing your goal and the process required to reach it prepares you for the expected—and unexpected—turns in the road. I lacked this short-term focus, and that probably hurt my chances of winning a gold medal.

FINDING YOUR FOCUS

Short-term focus is more Zen-oriented than logical. It means being able to clear your mind of everything extraneous and to concentrate on the task at hand. For instance, think about finishing the last 5 miles of the 60-mile training ride you're on instead of fretting about the upcoming century.

Successful short-term focus also means thinking only about cycling at crucial moments. It's letting yourself be of the moment and in the moment, and no place else.

Picture yourself riding in a group at a brisk pace, everyone close together. The pace is high. Every rider struggles to keep a uniform speed and ride a straight line. This is no time to have your mind on the argument you just had with your spouse (probably about going on this ride) or to contemplate the latest crisis at work.

In the most intense moments of cycling, the likelihood of making a mistake increases if you don't have complete focus. You may not even notice that your mind wanders at crucial times. On your next few rides, pay attention to how your mental state relates to various situations.

Studies have compared endurance athletes who zero in during races with those who zone out. Riders who zero in—who focus on the task at hand—perform better. This is called association. Disassociation is less productive because you take yourself out of the task rather than commit to it.

I'm not suggesting that you concentrate solely on cycling every minute of every ride. It's easy and natural to let your mind wander. In fact, it's often a healthy thing to do because cycling is such a good mental detox for stress.

I find that a good ride often begins with a warmup period to let the clutter sort itself in my head. Then I concentrate purely on the ride. Let your thoughts ramble early so that you get through this period. One reason I never use earphones—besides the fact that it's flat-out dangerous when you can't hear vehicles coming from behind—is that music distracts from thinking about the ride.

DRIVEN TO GRIN

As I discovered in my racing career, learning to focus certainly improves performance. But there's another benefit to acquiring this ability.

Think about the principle in less-competitive terms. You power-eat your lunch while you're reading the paper, the stereo is on, and the kids are running around the kitchen. As you put your plate in the sink, you realize that you didn't even taste the food because of all the distractions. Then you spoon out some ice cream that you've been craving. As you start to eat, all else is forgotten, and the sweet taste becomes your focus. It's the most delicious bowl of ice cream you've ever had. You savor every bite.

The point is that the more concentrated your focus is, the more concentrated your pleasure is. This is absolutely true in cycling. The times that I've felt most alive have been during and right after a period of absolute focus.

To train your concentration on specific aspects of cycling, do mental intervals. Focus on your breathing for 1 minute, then focus on your pedaling for 1 minute. As with any interval workout, rest between concentration periods.

As I trained my mind to concentrate, my results improved. But an unexpected bonus came directly following an especially intense finish, when a smile would instantly crease my face and a feeling of exhilaration would take over. I started calling this feeling the grin factor.

Grinning isn't exactly a scientific measuring device, but it is an accurate gauge of how much fun something is. Think of ripping on a descent, going faster than you previously dared, on the edge but in control. When you reach the bottom, you punch a fist in the air and shout. Or you're spinning along in a paceline where everyone rides in sync. The miles fly by. When the group pulls into the customary water stop, everyone beams and starts talking at once.

The grin can be subtle, too. Maybe you are rolling along by yourself on a road that you've ridden many times, but on this day you notice everything: the color of the sky, the scent in the air, the sound of your tires on the pavement. You feel a smile, perhaps bigger inside than outside.

With my competitive days behind me, the grin factor has become even more important. It's what I love about cycling, and it's possible only through focus.

FIVE

Year-Round
Improvement

COME IN FROM THE COLD

By Fred Matheny

No matter where you live, it's tough to ride in winter. Even if snow and ice aren't covering the roads, subzero windchills make cycling plenty risky. In more temperate areas long spells of cold rain may be your nemesis. And even on a nice day in Miami or San Diego, the sun sets a lot earlier, reducing the amount of daylight to the point where it's hard to fit rides in on weekdays.

But even in the most inhospitable places on Earth, cycling is always possible. Set your bike on an indoor trainer and nothing can stop you from retaining last summer's fitness and preparing for next spring's challenges. Done right, three or four weekly rides to nowhere can actually increase your power and speed.

The enemy is boredom. You can defeat it with variety. See "Spinning Your Wheels" on page 124 for five workouts that help you conquer brain drain as you boost your fitness level.

INDOOR CYCLING STRATEGIES

As you pedal in place, try these tips to keep your indoor workout comfortable and fun.

Get some air. In a room with no air circulation, you will generate an enormous amount of body heat on an indoor trainer. Create an artificial headwind by placing a large box fan 3 feet in front of your face. Still dripping? Wear sweatbands on your forehead and wrists and keep a towel and dry T-shirt handy.

Drink up. Fluids are important to keep your core temperature down and to replace the energy you're burning—and that applies whether

Make indoor cycling more pleasant with music and a fan.

you are indoors or on the road. Drink at least one bottle of cold sports drink during a 45-minute indoor session.

Be brief. There's no reason to grind away on the trainer, trying to build endurance. You can get a great indoor workout in less than an hour. Wait until you are back on the road to do long rides.

Go for a change of pace. Beat boredom by doing something different every minute or two. Stand up, change gears, increase your cadence, alternate hand positions, pedal with one foot while resting the other on a stool—anything to add variety and help make the time go faster.

Look and listen. Some riders prefer listening to Pearl Jam, while others like watching a bike race video. Why not try both together? Give yourself some serious sensory input. Music and images can be motivational, and they'll take your mind off how slow the clock is moving.

(continued on page 126)

SPINNING YOUR WHEELS

Don't let foul weather dampen your training program. Instead, try one of the following workouts, which have been customized for indoor rides. They are adapted from *Smart Cycling* by Arnie Baker, M.D., a several-time national masters champion and a member of *Bicycling* magazine's fitness advisory board.

Note that the gear recommendations are based on the common 39/53-tooth chainring combination and a cassette with these cogs: 13T, 15T, 17T, 19T, and 21T. If your gearing differs, use something similar, but pay close attention to your perceived exertion to be sure you are not overdoing it (or underdoing it). And if there is no cadence indicator on your cycle's computer, count pedal revolutions for 15 seconds and multiply by four to determine revolutions per minute (rpm).

Min.	Activity
	WORKOUT 1: VARIETY
0–3	Warm up in the 39 × 21T gear. Start at 70 rpm and increase by 10 rpm each minute.
3–6	Shift to 39 × 19T. Pedal at 70 rpm and increase to 100 rpm for 15 seconds to end each minute.
6–9	Shift to 53 × 17T and stand for 1 minute. Then shift to 39 × 19T and sit for 1 minute. Then shift back to 53 × 17T and stand for 1 minute.
9–12	Shift to 53 × 19T. Alternate between 100 rpm and 70 rpm every 30 seconds.
12–20	In 39 × 19T, pedal with one leg for 1 minute. Switch legs each minute.
20–23	Spin easily in 39 × 19T.
23–33	Ride hard in 53 × 17T for 1 minute, then spin easily in 39 × 17T for 1 minute. Repeat five times.
33–41	Sprint in 53 × 15T for 15 seconds, then pedal easily in 39 × 19T for 45 seconds. Repeat eight times.
41–45	Cool down by pedaling gently for just over 1 minute each in 39 × 17T, 19T, and 21T.
	WORKOUT 2: TIME TRIAL
0–12	Warm up as in Workout 1.
12–17	Shift to 53 × 19T and pedal steadily at 90 to 100 rpm.
17–21	Spin easily in 39 × 19T.
21–26	Shift to 53 × 17T and ride hard at 90 to 100 rpm.
26–31	Spin easily in 39 × 19T.

Min.	Activity
31–41	Shift to 53 × 17T or 15T and ride hard at 90 to 100 rpm.
41–45	Cool down by spinning easily in 39 × 21T.

Workout 3: Sprint

0–12	Warm up as in Workout 1.
12–22	Shift to 39 × 17T and spin at 100-plus rpm for 10 seconds. Then pedal slowly for 50 seconds. Repeat 10 times.
22–27	Pedal slowly in 39 × 19T.
27–37	Shift to 53 × 19T and sprint all-out for 10 seconds. Then pedal slowly in 39 × 19T for 50 seconds. Repeat 10 times.
37–45	Cool down by spinning easily in 39 × 21T.

Workout 4: Hill Climb

0–12	Warm up as in Workout 1.
12–14	Shift to 53 × 19T and ride for 2 minutes at 80 rpm.
14–16	Recover in 39 × 19T.
16–18	Shift to 53 × 17T and ride for 2 minutes at 80 rpm.
18–20	Recover in 39 × 19T.
20–22	Shift to 53 × 15T and ride for 2 minutes at 80 rpm.
22–24	Recover in 39 × 19T.
24–26	Shift to 53 × 13T and ride for 2 minutes. Tired yet? Don't let your cadence drop below 70 rpm.
26–32	Recover in 39 × 19T. (You've earned it!)
32–42	Shift to 53 × 13T. Ride hard at 80 rpm for 1 minute. Recover for 1 minute in 39 × 21T. Repeat 10 times.
42–45	Cool down by spinning easily in 39 × 21T.

Workout 5: Recovery

0–12	Warm up as in Workout 1.
12–17	Spin easily in 39 × 17T while listening to two favorite songs.
17–27	Spin in 39 × 15T while watching television.
27–32	Spin fast in 39 × 17T while listening to fast-paced music.
32–42	Spin easily in 39 × 17T while watching Tour de France videos or talking on the phone.
42–45	Cool down in 39 × 21T to one of your favorite tunes.

Perhaps the ultimate antidote to boredom is the CompuTrainer. This high-tech system holds your bike and has a control panel that connects to a television screen through a modified Nintendo unit. It charts your heart rate, power output, calorie consumption, cadence, time, distance, speed, and average speed. You can race against an electronic opponent or your previous performances on famous road courses. You can also design your own killer loop, putting in climbs and headwinds. The trainer automatically adjusts rolling resistance to simulate the terrain you see on the screen. It makes you change gears and pedaling force, just like outside.

SIMPLIFIED WEIGHT TRAINING

By Fred Matheny

I have heard all the excuses for not lifting weights. It takes too much time. Gym memberships are expensive. Exposing a cyclist's body in the iron-pumpers' lair is intimidating.

But weight training works. According to Chris Carmichael, former U.S. national coaching director, Lance Armstrong lifted during the winter of 1994–95, then astounded the pro peloton with his performance in the spring classics and his domination of the Tour DuPont. Teammate Axel Merckx, who blossomed into a top rider in 1996, also spent off-season time in the weight room.

Pumping iron isn't just good for racing. It's healthful, too. In a study at West Virginia University in Morgantown, researchers comparing weight training to aerobic workouts found that both produce similar cardiac benefits. Lifting helps retain muscle volume as you age so that you can ride fast and strong for years to come. Added strength also protects against injury.

Best of all, this miracle is easy to achieve. All it takes is an hour each week and a small equipment expenditure. Here's how to do it right.

Learn proper form. To avoid injury and speed progress, do the exercises correctly. If you don't know how, nothing beats personal instruction. Consult a local weight-training coach certified by the National Strength and Conditioning Association (NSCA). Or watch the excellent instructional video "Strength Training for Cyclists" by Harvey Newton, program director for NSCA in Colorado Springs, Colorado.

Do your homework. Work out at home to increase convenience and decrease expense. For body-weight exercises you need only a door-mounted chinning bar, two sturdy chairs for dips, and enough floor

A WORKOUT FOR EVERY BODY

This streamlined weight-training schedule won't make you look like Arnold. But you'll ride a little more like Lance.

Strengthening Phase:
November through March

Two or three times per week (but not on consecutive days), do one to three sets in each of these five areas.

1. Upper-body pushing exercise, such as push-ups, bench presses, or dips

2. Upper-body pulling exercise, such as pull-ups, bent rows, or upright rows

3. Abdominal exercise, such as crunches

4. Lower-back exercise, such as back extensions

5. Leg exercise, such as step-ups, lunges, or light squats

Maintenance Phase:
April through October

Two times per week (preferably after an easy ride), do one set in each of these four areas.

1. Push-ups, bench presses, or dips

2. Pull-ups, bent rows, or upright rows

3. Crunches

4. Back extensions

space to do push-ups and crunches. If you add a light barbell set, a bench, and a sturdy platform for step-ups, you can work virtually any muscle group.

Rise to the challenge. Adhere to the progressive resistance principle. That is, as your body adapts to a training load, you must increase resistance to continue improving. When you can do a set of 10 to 12 repetitions of an exercise comfortably, increase the amount of weight, the number of reps, or the number of sets.

Of course, you can't improve forever. During winter, lift two or three days each week and aim for strength gains. Then to retain the strength you have built as you begin riding more in the spring, lift once or twice per week and don't worry about pushing the intensity.

Time it right. Lift after easy rides when you are warmed up but not tired. Include gentle stretching and light calisthenics. About 20 minutes in winter and 10 to 15 minutes in summer should suffice for the whole routine—if you keep moving and don't waste time between sets or exercises.

Get a leg up on training. During spring and summer, riding usually provides enough work for your legs. If you want more, try "squats" on the bike, using a slightly larger than normal gear on climbs or when riding into the wind. (Be sure to warm up carefully before doing this. And don't try it if you have knee trouble.) In winter, simple exercises, such as lunges and step-ups, can keep your quads strong while you cross-train with running, skiing, and other aerobic activities.

Remember the reason. You're a cyclist, not a lifter. Don't forget this. Regularity beats volume. It's better to lift a little each week for the rest of your life than overdose on iron, get sick of it, and quit in disgust.

A NEW VIEW OF CROSS-TRAINING

By Davis Phinney

For top cyclists, cross-training during the racing season has always been taboo. I was raised with the old-world notion that the best and only thing a rider should do is ride. And ride more. This is called specificity. The old guard advocated being as true to the pedaling action as possible. I followed this tenet for much of my career, as do many professional racers today.

But being one-dimensional has its downside. Some cyclists become so specialized that a run through the airport to catch a plane can cause incredible muscle soreness. And they call themselves athletes?

As a retired pro, I no longer ride big miles, lacking both time and motivation. But I do stay fit by doing something aerobic almost every day. I have found that by mixing sports wisely, I feel as good on the bike as I ever have. And my hunger to ride has increased. Having discovered these benefits, I now urge riders to include other sports right from the start of their cycling careers.

CONFESSIONS OF A CONVERT

When I was younger, I ate, drank, and breathed cycling. It permeated me. There were quite a few activities that I stopped because they were not specific to bike riding. This made me supremely fit—but only when turning the pedals.

Then when I was injured in a race in Sicily, I discovered that although I wasn't able to pedal, I could ski. This was in March, when there was plenty of snow in the Italian mountains. Desperate for activity, I borrowed some cross-country skis and took off. After three weeks of this—and no riding—I jumped back on the bike with good overall fitness. Later that summer, I won a stage in the Tour de France. Still, it didn't dawn on me that maybe this bike-specific thing was overrated.

During my last few pro seasons, I skied quite a bit during the winter. The cardiovascular benefit improved my climbing, while the overall body strength improved my general riding style. Taking this a step further, I borrowed a rowing machine and used it during the season. Instead of a complete rest day, I would do an easy rowing workout. This served to get the blood flowing and work muscles that were not fatigued.

In hindsight I realized that being specific isn't the only way and that cross-training should be more than an off-season tool. As the blinders loosened, a world of opportunity unfolded. I realized that running, hiking, swimming, rowing, in-line skating, roller skiing, and other aerobic activities could supply big benefits.

EXPLORE YOUR OPTIONS

One major attribute of cross-training is the development of aerobic and anaerobic pathways. Think of your arterial system, which takes oxygen from your lungs and energy from various sources, as a series of small roads working perfectly with no gridlock points. This concept has been the foundation of the argument for being sport-specific. You must refine the pathways to the muscle groups that cycling involves.

One side effect, however, is that these muscle groups become overworked. This is when cross-training can help. Because cyclists tend to work one muscle group day after day, complete recovery rarely occurs. Cross-training can be rejuvenating and help rest those tired muscle groups (not to mention a tired psyche). Instead of slogging along day after day with dead legs, you can still burn fat, get that all-important endorphin boost, and then climb on the bike feeling fresh and strong. The payoff for me was being able to push a big gear. The strength this takes is the first thing that goes with chronic fatigue.

When looking at your training plan, categorize what you do as being cycling-specific or not. Cycling-specific means riding on-road, off-road, cyclocross, or on a stationary trainer. Training that is noncycling-specific generally involves endurance-based activities, but without the same mechanics as riding.

Evaluate your options. What do you like to do? What do you miss when you are cycling? Here are some suggestions.

Running. One of my former team directors, Mike Neel, says that running is the best way to strengthen your tendons and connective tissues.

It develops the powerful levering action of your ankle, which can benefit your pedal stroke. Also, it's hard to train your cardiovascular system on the bike if your legs are tired from lots of riding. Because running uses different muscles, you can get the aerobic benefit and give your cycling muscles a break. Running is great for anaerobic threshold work, too. Because it requires you to carry your weight, it puts your system under immediate stress. And, of course, when you are on a tight schedule, running is a time-saver. A little goes a long way. And it doesn't require much equipment.

The downside is the potential for injury. I started by using a treadmill with a suspended base that reduced impact stress. This led me to trail running, which is softer and less likely to cause injury. I'm now able to run on pavement, which is great when traveling.

Swimming. This was frowned upon in the old days because it was said to be bad for your muscles. Now triathletes have shown that it has no negative effects. And world sprint champion Marty Nothstein uses swimming workouts as part of his off-season program, something unheard of in past years. He combines pool sessions with weight workouts and stationary cycling, obtaining aerobic benefits while reducing the stress on his muscles.

Swimming allows you to maintain or improve certain aspects of your physiology. It tones and strengthens your upper body, giving balance to your physique. It is great for anyone who wants to develop a stronger torso and shoulders. Swimming also stretches and elongates your leg muscles, unlike the confining motion of pedaling. It is so gentle that it rarely makes you stiff or sore.

The downside is that you need a place to swim, which may require joining a health club. Then you have to work your schedule around the hours that it's open for lap swimming. While there is little risk of injury, you'll need to work on stroke mechanics, if you want to be efficient. Most clubs and some communities have swim programs with coaches and great camaraderie.

Skiing and skating. As mentioned, cross-country skiing—either the traditional diagonal stride or skating—is a great complement to bike riding. Along with speed skating, it has probably been used by more cyclists throughout history than any other off-season activity. Additionally, roller skiing and in-line skating are fantastic summer diversions. (I recommend poles with either activity to take some stress off your legs and involve your upper body.) These are ways to enjoy the roads in a whole different way. Because they are relatively gentle, low-impact activities (unless you fall), they don't require a lengthy break-in period. As with running you carry your weight and use the major muscle groups to stress your cardiovascular system.

Cyclocross. This sport, in which you ride part of a course and run tougher sections with your bike on your shoulder, is becoming more popular in the United States. Europeans have enjoyed it for decades, with many road racers taking part. It's a great workout because you are pedaling, running, jumping obstacles, and handling and carrying your machine. Some bike clubs have fall and winter cyclocross series, and there are even national championship races. Cyclocross is so much fun that you forget that you are working out—until later in the day, when every muscle is mellow with fatigue.

Indoor training. There are various options when you can't get outside. For example, in my basement I have a small workout room. It includes a stationary trainer for the bike, a rowing machine, and a treadmill. When the weather is bad or I can't get to the health club, just hitting "the room" makes my day. It has been my salvation on many occasions, helping fulfill goals that are important to my mental and physical health. Sweating and burning calories supplies the bridge that I need until the next time I can hit the road.

HIT THE DIRT

By Fred Matheny

I f you're a dedicated road rider, your opinion of mountain biking may not be very high. After all, off-road riding is dirty, abusive, relatively slow, and attractive to people with more holes in their bodies than Dennis Rodman. But take it from me, a roadie long before the first clunker hit the trail, mountain biking is also fun and rewarding. Off-road riding can pay big dividends if your goal is to be the best pavement-pounder possible.

Consider this: Most recreational cyclists lack two major skills—climbing and cornering. It's relatively easy to improve in both of these areas by riding a mountain bike, something that top U.S. roadies have been including in their winter training programs for several years. Recreational cyclists who can only envy the acrobatic bike handling and overwhelming power of top racers can use off-road riding to develop these talents.

BIKE ACROBATICS

Riding a fat-tired mountain bike on trails will do wonders for your ability to stay upright on two wheels. Navigating through icy ruts, powering up muddy hills, and slithering down steep embankments put a premium on body control, balance, and a feel for the limitations of a bicycle in the presence of gravity. No matter how skilled you are at keeping the rubber on the pavement, there will always be challenges: lousy drivers, snarling dogs, slippery corners. Riding a mountain bike on dirt, snow, mud, or grass is the best and safest way to improve balance and control. You will learn to handle far more difficult terrain than you will probably ever meet on asphalt.

Some off-road cyclists develop a wizard's bicycle-handling touch. On a mountain bike you often lose traction in corners, so you get used to the feeling of sliding. You learn to not panic, to stay loose when the rear tire is traveling sideways. Then when the same thing happens on the road, you don't freak out and dump it. This art can be honed to a high degree. Some cyclists who combine road and off-road racing are comfortable skidding their skinny tires through wet downhill corners on high-speed descents.

You can develop bike-handling skills faster off-road because the penalty for a crash is usually less severe. Soft dirt is a lot more forgiving than blacktop. You learn how far you can lean in a corner only by pushing closer and closer to the edge until you eventually crash. That sort of experimentation just isn't done on the road—at least not willingly. Therefore you can only guess where the limits are. If you are on a grassy field or soft dirt path, however, you can be more daring with less fear. The result is a faster learning curve without undue risk of injury.

POWER PLUS

Fat, knobby off-road tires produce extra rolling resistance on even the firmest surfaces. Add mud, sand, or snow to an uphill grade, and suddenly, the killer hills on your road rides will seem much less formidable. You don't need big dirt hills either. Even a gentle grade can be demanding when gravity is in league with a quagmire. Riding regularly through the glop can start you on the way to power that cracks crankarms and crushes cassettes.

Riding off-road also strengthens your upper body as you pull on the handlebar to conquer hills and lurch over obstacles. A disadvantage of road cycling as a builder of fitness is that it emphasizes the legs and shortchanges the upper body. This isn't true of off-road riding. Many newcomers to mountain bikes comment that their arms and shoulders get as tired as their legs. Strength above the waist makes you a more powerful climber and sprinter, and it helps prevent injury to your shoulder area should you fall.

Don't forget variety. Many roadies train on the same courses all racing season. On a mountain bike the number of possible training routes is almost infinite. Dirt and gravel roads, towpaths, rail-trails, jeep roads, parks—they are all open for exploration. When you get jaded with pavement and civilization, go take a ride in the dirt.

And there is a final advantage. Despite rocks, stumps, and overhanging tree limbs, mountain biking is actually not as dangerous as pedaling along a city street. Unpaved roads are much less traveled by motor vehicles, so you can forget about traffic congestion and just enjoy your ride.

It doesn't take a major investment to get all these benefits if you already have a mountain bike. If you don't, the payoff in fun and fitness makes the purchase of a new or used machine well worth it. Remember, to be the best road rider possible, you need to spend some time off-road.

TAKE TO THE TRAIL

To get the power and bike-handling benefits of off-road cycling while avoiding injury, good riding position is essential. Your pedaling efficiency will increase, and your risk of knee problems will decrease, if you approximate the saddle position that you use on your road bike on your mountain bike. Some roadies install a drop handlebar with bar-end shifters so that their mountain bikes are even closer to their road bikes, but most coaches say this isn't necessary. It's more important to duplicate saddle height than upper-body position.

Be careful not to use gears that are too large. Plodding uphill at 40 revolutions per minute will prevent you from developing maximum power, and it may destroy your knees. Choose gears low enough to let you spin over the tough spots. Even strong cyclists in the mountain bike mecca of Crested Butte, Colorado, often have a granny chainring of 26 or 24 teeth.

A mountain bike set up like your road bike also works great for road training in early-season rain or slush. The sealed bearings resist moisture and mud, and the earth-mover tires rarely puncture. In fact, if you need one more good excuse to buy a mountain bike, think of all the wear and tear you'll save on your road bike in lousy weather.

Be sure to mix mountain biking and road riding wisely, however. It's easy to lose the snap and spin that good roadies must have if you do too much power-intensive trail riding. It can turn you into a plodder on pavement. If you balance the two types of riding, though, you can enjoy extra power development and still retain your leg speed.

TRAINING WHEELS

You can reap the benefits of off-road riding without structured workouts. You will learn most necessary bike-handling skills by haphazardly meandering on trails and through the brush while having fun. If the terrain in your area isn't too severe, you can increase the difficulty simply by increasing the speed.

Or you can set up a more formal practice area. In fact, it may be worth your time to attend a mountain bike circuit race, just to get an idea of the obstacles these cyclists contend with. The ideal: a challenging 1- to 3-mile circuit that begins about 5 miles from your house. You can warm up on the way, ride the circuit for 30 to 60 minutes while throwing in all the variations that the terrain and topography allow, then cool down on the way home.

The ideal course includes at least one long, steady climb; several short, abrupt hills; tight corners; and some flat sections. The idea is to challenge all your abilities each time around.

Don't ride the circuit the same way every time—always pushing the hills and cruising the flats, for instance. Instead, use the terrain in the way a good downhill skier works the moguls. Bang up a hill in a big gear one time, finesse it the next. Take a corner at high speed on the most efficient line, then try a more difficult line and see if you can get yourself into and out of trouble. Ride the course in each direction to create different challenges.

Don't be limited to naturally occurring features either. Roll logs or rocks onto the trail, creating obstacles you must jump over. Bunny-hopping is a skill that comes in very handy on the road when you are forced into the curb or over a pothole. (To learn how to execute a bunnyhop, see chapter 20.)

Once you have a good off-road circuit, don't keep it a secret. Because bike-handling skills change in a pack, ride the loop with three or four friends. Stay close together and jostle each other on the flats. Try to sneak through corners with an inside line. Purposely touch wheels to learn the correct reaction. Some crashes are inevitable in this sort of training, so wear your helmet, gloves, and thick clothing. A few bruises are a small price to pay for the vastly increased confidence and pack-riding skills that you'll gain.

Do a mountain bike workout twice a week in winter and early spring. You'll see a big improvement in your skills when the road season gets underway. But even while the season is in full swing, it's smart to head for the dirt periodically to sharpen your reflexes and add fun to your training routine.

33

FROM OFF-ROAD TO ASPHALT

By Ed Pavelka

During the past decade, millions of people have come into cycling on mountain bikes. If you're one of them and you're still unsure about buying a road bike, here are some ways to turn your off-road machine into a worthy pavement-pounder and get greater efficiency and speed when riding road events. But before you start overhauling your bike, add up the cost of the modifications you choose. If the total approaches the price of a good-quality road bike (used or new), it may make sense to buy one and leave your mountain bike dirt-ready. Then you'll have the right machines to enjoy almost any type of cycling.

Handlebar. For road riding you need a longer and lower upper-body position than your mountain bike allows. This position reduces wind resistance and improves weight distribution, which helps keep you comfortable in the saddle. You also need the ability to change your hand positions and back angle to ward off fatigue. All of these things can be inexpensively accomplished by installing bar-ends. These extensions cost about $20 to $50 per pair, depending on material and features. You can easily install them yourself, saving labor charges. Once in place, they give you a position similar to gripping the brake hoods of a road bike. This is a big help when standing to climb or for reducing your frontal area in a headwind. Leave them on full-time for the same benefits off-road.

An even bigger boost to comfort and aerodynamics comes from a bolt-on aero bar. This takes all the pressure off your hands and automatically raises cruising speed by 1 to 2 miles per hour for most riders. You'll see pricey aero bars with trick features, but all you need for oc-

Easy modifications make a mountain bike fit for the road.

casional mountain bike (or hybrid) modification is a basic model. Profile and Scott make good ones for about $50.

Wheels. No matter what else you do, lose those knobbies. Wide, low-pressure, lug-tread tires are slow and noisy on pavement, and they corner poorly. Replace them with narrower, smooth-tread rubber from a top company such as Continental, Specialized, or Ritchey. Use light-weight tubes, too. Inflate them to 100 pounds per square inch and your bike will be noticeably faster and more lively, with hundreds of grams less wheel weight. Expect to pay $16 to $35 apiece for these tires.

If you're really committed, consider a separate pair of 26-inch road wheels. These can save you changeover time and more weight. A newer option is Spinergy's Rev-X-Roks composite wheel. These four-spoke beauties are tough enough for off-road abuse, and they'll give you an aerodynamic advantage at road speeds. They're pricey at about $700 per pair, but Spinergy provides a low-price replacement policy if they become damaged.

Other parts. Consider a clipless pedal system if your bike is equipped with plain pedals or clips and straps. Clipless systems are lighter, more efficient, and easy to use. They work equally well on- and off-road. Expect to pay at least $50 for a pair.

You probably won't need a stock mountain bike's super-low gears on the road. Install a set of tighter-ratio cogs to get more usable gears and smaller difference between them. This will improve your efficiency by helping you maintain your best pedal cadence. A typical Shimano cassette costs around $30.

For long rides on- or off-road, it helps to have extra liquid and a way to carry spare gear. The $8 Mega Block, a rubber bracket and strap, installs to the frame in seconds without tools and lets you carry a water bottle, U-lock, pump, light battery, and other accessories on any bike. For bigger loads consider a cantilever rear rack. This type attaches to the seatpost only (no struts), so it easily fits bikes with rear suspensions and those without dropout eyelets. Made by various companies, these run from $35 to $60. On top, fasten a $30 to $45 trunk to carry extra food, rainwear, tools, and other gear.

SIX

Fueling
Your Engine

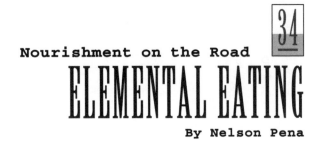

ELEMENTAL EATING

By Nelson Pena

In most recreational sports, eating is something you do afterward and, occasionally, beforehand. But in cycling, eating is often an important part of the activity. This is news to most beginning riders, and it's overlooked by many experienced riders. So let's get right to the basics. Here are the pertinent facts—the why, when, what, and how of eating, drinking, and cycling.

Q. Why do you need to eat and drink on the bike?

A. Food replenishes the energy burned while pedaling. Every time you eat something, your body takes the food's carbohydrate (natural compounds derived from starches and sugars) and stores it as fuel (glycogen) in your muscles. You have enough stored glycogen to provide energy for short rides. For longer efforts, however, you need to eat, or your glycogen stores will become depleted. When this occurs, less fuel reaches your brain and muscles, and you feel dizzy and tired. In running this is called hitting the wall. In cycling we call it bonking.

To avoid the bonk, carry something to eat if you will be riding for 90 minutes or longer. Also, never leave home without at least one full bottle. Cycling causes fluid loss, so you must protect yourself against dehydration and its debilitating effects.

Q. When should you eat and drink?

A. The oldest advice for cyclists is still the best advice: Drink before you're thirsty and eat before you're hungry. If you wait for your body to tell you that it needs nourishment, the energy won't be able to reach your muscles fast enough to help. One rule of thumb is to take a big swig from your bottle every 15 minutes. You should consume at least 20 ounces per hour, which is the content of one standard-size bottle. (Drink even more if the weather is hot and humid.) Another tenet is to allow yourself about an hour for digestion before riding. If you'll be cycling for more than 90 minutes, nibble during the ride. Avoid stuffing yourself at midride rest stops. Your digestive system requires a lot of blood to process such meals, which leaves less for delivering oxygen to your muscles.

Q. What should you eat and drink?

A. For fluid replacement on short rides, water works. But commercial sports drinks are better, especially on longer outings. This is because they replenish glycogen as well as lost liquid. Also, they are easier for the body to process than solid food. According to studies, cyclists can ride nearly 13 percent farther when ingesting a sports drink.

When you're not riding, your diet should be 60 to 70 percent carbohydrate, 20 to 30 percent fat, and 10 to 15 percent protein. High-carb foods include fruits, pasta, potatoes, rice, whole-grain breads, and vegetables.

Perhaps the most popular on-bike food is the banana. It is easy to eat, provides 105 calories of carbohydrate, and replaces potassium, an important element lost via sweating. Other fresh fruits such as pears (98 calories) and apples (81 calories) also provide carbohydrate, vitamins, minerals, and water—all necessary for good performance.

Some riders do well on higher-fat foods. Fat is accused of being an inefficient fuel source compared with carbohydrate, but it provides a longer burn that seems beneficial on rides that last several hours. Experiment to see how fat works for you. One easy-to-use source is an energy bar that provides a 40/30/30 ratio of carbohydrate, fat, and protein.

Many long-distance cyclists who ride at a steady, moderate pace mix nuts, raisins, M&Ms, whole-grain cereal or granola, and other favorite munchies into a personalized concoction called gorp (good ol' raisins and peanuts). This is easy to nibble and provides a steady flow of food energy.

Caffeine drinks (coffee, cola, or tea) may give you a temporary physical and mental boost. In several studies caffeine has been shown to promote the metabolism of fat for energy. But caffeine's beneficial

IS CYCLING MORE
THAN YOU CAN STOMACH?

For some riders, eating and drinking on long rides is easier said than done. They experience appetite loss—food just doesn't seem appealing—or they suffer digestion woes. Studies have shown that more than one-third of participants in exhausting endurance events experience one or more of these problems: inability to take in fluids or solids, heartburn, diarrhea, cramps, nausea, belching, vomiting, even internal bleeding.

The reason is that the gastrointestinal (GI) tract works differently during exercise. The stomach's emptying time slows, and its contents back up into the esophagus more readily. Stomach acid secretion decreases, while peristalsis—the action that moves food along—also changes. Most important, blood flow to the GI tract decreases by as much as 80 percent because more goes to your leg muscles. In fact, blood flow can decrease enough to cause bleeding of the bowel wall or stomach. (More blood means healthier tissue and, therefore, less bleeding.)

Meanwhile, dehydration sets up a vicious circle: The more dehydrated you are, the more you need fluids, yet the harder it is for the GI tract to accept them. (The stomach doesn't empty as well, which means the intestines have difficulty absorbing fluids.) Heat and humidity contribute to this problem, forcing the body to shunt blood to the skin to promote sweat and cooling. The result is less blood flow to the gut.

Ingesting fluids or solids that are hyperosmolar (more concentrated than blood) exacerbates the problem. Before concentrated fluids can be absorbed, they must be diluted until they match the concentration of blood. This means that the walls of the gut must secrete fluid into the GI tract, often causing cramps, a tight feeling, and diarrhea. So a sports drink may actually contribute to the misery. Although fructose (fruit sugar) has important performance-enhancing properties, fruit juices or sodas containing fructose may be more difficult to tolerate than sports drinks containing glucose (table sugar).

As if all this weren't enough, some people find that fiber, fat, protein,

effects are reduced if you become a routine user, and it also contributes to the risk of dehydration by encouraging fluid loss through frequent urination.

Q. How do you eat while riding?

A. The best place to carry food is in the rear pockets of your jersey. To reach for, say, a banana, first grip the handlebar with one hand next caffeine, alcohol, or anxiety before a big event can increase their troubles. This is a lot to overcome, so here are some tips.

Go easy at first. Increased intensity worsens the gut's function, so don't start too hard. When doing a century, for instance, you should begin drinking and eating before the halfway point, so it makes sense to keep your pace below 75 percent of maximum heart rate for the first few hours.

Get wet early. Remember dehydration's vicious circle? Don't let it start. Begin drinking 15 minutes into the ride.

Stay cool. The stomach empties faster with cool liquids than it does with warm or air-temperature ones. Also, sugar and electrolytes improve taste. It's easy to prove this to yourself. After a long, hot ride, look at a warm jug of water. Then consider a big, refrigerated bottle of sports drink. Which is more appealing?

Don't concentrate. A 5 percent glucose solution empties from the stomach about five times faster than a 40 percent solution.

Learn what works for you. Some riders have success with certain drinks, while others try them and cramp. Use training rides to determine what works for you. Full-strength fruit juices, some full-strength energy drinks, and fatty meals almost universally cause problems. Caffeine may help some riders perform better, but it causes GI symptoms in others. Never experiment during a big event.

Control nervous jitters. Easier said than done, right? For new riders, pre-event stomach flutters may simply disappear after completing an event or two. Riders who can't get over their nervousness may benefit from seeing a sports psychologist, who can help them channel it.

Shape up. Training improves your stomach's ability to function at a given workload. In other words, if you're fit, a smaller percentage of your oxygen uptake is required by working muscles, making it more available for digestion in the GI tract.

—Arnie Baker, M.D.

to the stem to hold the bike steady. Then reach around with the other hand to grab the banana, which you can then partially peel with your hand or teeth and eat. Store the remainder in its peel until you want more.

Many cyclists develop the ability to ride no-handed in order to sit up, take out food, open it, eat it, and stash the remainder while cruising down a smooth road. Another approach is to grab a bite while pausing at intersections or overlooks. It's also common for cyclists to stash food in seat bags or rack trunks for devouring at spontaneous roadside picnics.

Finally, don't forget the postride meal. As a cyclist, you will regularly burn hundreds if not thousands of calories while exercising. So when you get home, you can guiltlessly enjoy an extra helping of your favorite food. In fact, eating a carbohydrate-rich meal within an hour after finishing is the most effective way to replenish glycogen stores for the next day's ride. Just try to make sure that indulgence doesn't include a fat-laden choice, such as a plate of french fries or a piece of chocolate cake.

How to Avoid Dehydration
WET YOUR WHISTLE

By Julie Walsh

It doesn't supply calories, vitamins, or minerals, yet water is essential for virtually every bodily function. It aids digestion, cushions organs, and keeps your body temperature from rising to lethal levels during exercise. In fact, H_2O is so important that it accounts for 55 to 65 percent of your weight.

When you are cycling, your muscles produce 30 to 100 times more heat than when you are at rest. The body extinguishes this inferno primarily by increasing sweat rate. In summer, you can lose more than 2 liters (about 67 ounces) of fluids per hour on a really hot day. If you don't replace it, your power output declines in about 30 minutes. A study of trained cyclists found that they could barely finish a 2-hour ride at 65 percent of maximum oxygen capacity without fluids. In ultramarathon events dehydration and saddle sores are the leading reasons riders drop out, according to Arnie Baker, M.D., a champion cyclist and member of Bicycling magazine's fitness advisory board.

Studies by Edward Coyle, Ph.D., director of the human performance laboratory at the University of Texas at Austin, reveal that cyclists who lose a quart of fluid experience a rise in heart rate of eight beats per minute, a decrease in cardiac function, and an increase in body temperature. Dehydration, says Dr. Coyle, may cause increased metabolic stress on muscles and faster glycogen depletion. It also wreaks havoc on your internal thermostat by decreasing blood flow to the skin, slowing your sweat rate, and increasing the time needed for fluids to be absorbed into the bloodstream. What's worse, by the time you feel thirsty, your body has already lost up to 2 percent of its weight—about a quart of fluid.

Conventional wisdom says to drink eight 8-ounce glasses of fluids daily, but that's for nonexercising couch potatoes. Cyclists have different fluid needs depending on fitness, gender, body size, and conditions. A rule of thumb is to drink 1 milliliter of fluid for every calorie you burn, says Mitch Kanter, Ph.D., director of the Gatorade Sport Science Institute in Barrington, Illinois. "At about 3,500 calories a day, you'll need around 3½ liters. That's 14½ (8-ounce) glasses of fluid." He advises, however, that it's best to gauge hydration by monitoring five simple markers.

O Do you urinate less than three times during a normal workday?

O Is your urine dark yellow? Does it have a strong odor?

O Do you get headaches toward the end of a long ride or shortly afterward?

O Do you drink less than one water bottle per hour while riding?

O Do you lose more than 2 pounds during rides?

If you answer yes to any of these questions, your body is heading for a drought.

WAYS TO STAY AFLOAT

Does your mouth feel dry just reading this? Here are six ways to beat the dehydration monster.

Fill up beforehand. Drink plenty of fluids every day. Then for a race, long ride, or tour, start hyper-hydrating at least 24 hours in advance. Many pro cyclists carry water bottles all day during the racing season to stay fully hydrated. Avoid drinks containing alcohol or caffeine because both act as mild diuretics, causing the body to excrete more fluid. If you have trouble meeting your calorie needs, use sports drinks, recovery drinks, or other liquid supplements. If you are weight-conscious, quaff no-calorie or low-calorie fluids such as water, seltzer, diet soda, and diluted fruit juice.

Set a schedule. To negate fluid loss via sweat, practice drinking strategies during training. Determine your sweat rate per hour by weighing yourself before and after rides. (Every pound lost equals 16 ounces of fluid.) Then figure out how much fluid your stomach can tolerate per hour and the best drinking schedule to replace it. Set your sports watch to alert you to drink 4 to 8 ounces every 15 minutes, regardless of whether you are thirsty, Dr. Kanter recommends. It takes practice to drink more than a quart per hour without intestinal discomfort. A hydration system that you wear like a backpack, such as those made by CamelBak and Blackburn, provides plenty of easily accessible water, so you'll drink more.

Replenish your supply. After you have ridden for several hours, pump down more fluids. What you drink makes a difference. In a study Dr. Coyle had dehydrated athletes drink nearly 2 liters of diet cola, water, or sports drink 2 hours after they exercised, then compared the effects. He found that diet cola replenished 54 percent of the fluid loss; water, 64 percent; and sports drink, 69 percent.

Snack on something salty. Sodium makes your blood spongelike so that you absorb more water and excrete less. "Each liter of sweat saps between 500 and 1,000 or more milligrams of sodium," notes Lawrence Armstrong, Ph.D., of the human performance laboratory at the University of Connecticut in Storrs.

Athletes should drink plentifully with meals and snacks because food naturally contains many times more sodium than sports drinks or energy bars, suggests Dr. Coyle.

Choose juicy foods. Around 60 percent of your daily fluid comes from the foods you eat, but some foods increase hydration better than others. For instance, fruits and vegetables are great fluid sources—they are 80 to 95 percent water by weight. Eating the recommended five to nine daily servings of produce means that you will get a lot of extra water in your diet. If you are downing protein supplements, you should drink even more. "You'll need more water to metabolize and excrete the extra protein," Dr. Kanter says. Fat and water don't readily mix, so many high-fat foods provide little additional fluid, he adds.

Be a sport. Most popular sports drinks contain sodium, potassium, and other electrolytes as well as energy-producing carbohydrates. These drinks are recommended for exercise lasting more than 1 hour. Whenever you plan to cycle for several hours, make sure you have two bottles of your favorite brand. Sports drinks are also useful for shorter workouts that include high-intensity riding such as sprints and intervals.

Whatever you choose, make sure you like the way it tastes so that you'll be motivated to drink. Also, cool fluids taste better and may be absorbed more rapidly than warm ones. Riders should carry two bottles—one chilled and one frozen, says Edmund R. Burke, Ph.D., associate professor of exercise science at the University of Colorado in Colorado Springs, and an exercise physiologist who has worked with the U.S. national cycling team since the mid-1970s. As you drink from the first bottle, the frozen one melts, so the liquid is cold when you need it.

FAST FOOD

By Jo Ostgarden

A s you now know, your energy supply must be restocked after a couple of hours of cycling. That's roughly how long it takes to exhaust carbohydrate stores. But what if you have already devoured the contents of your jersey pockets and you still have miles to ride?

Get thee to a convenience store or fast-food restaurant, and soon. (You won't have far to look in most parts of the civilized world.) Traditionally considered nutritional junkyards, these places are actually carbohydrate gold mines in disguise—if you know which foods to choose.

CONVENIENCE STORES

Scan the aisles carefully and you'll find an assortment of high-octane fuels ranging from burritos to energy bars to sports drinks. The key is to select foods containing at least 60 percent carbohydrate and no more than 30 percent fat.

Here are 10 finds, all of which follow good nutrition guidelines.

Chicken burritos. Many stores have microwave ovens for cooking the packaged burritos you'll find in the cooler. Not all burritos are created equal, though; many are stuffed with fat. Your best chance is to find Don Miguel's half-pound chicken burrito or a similar brand. It offers 360 calories, 54 grams of carbohydrate (60 percent of total calories), 17 grams of protein, and 8 grams of fat (just 20 percent of total calories). Avoid beef burritos, which can be as much as 60 percent fat.

Fruit-flavored yogurt. Check the dairy cooler for this deluxe carb item. Be sure to pick one of the low-fat varieties. A typical 1-cup serving contains 250 calories, 45 grams of carbohydrate (72 percent), 10 grams of protein, and 2.5 grams of fat (9 percent). Combine it with a one-serving box of cereal for more flavor—and more carbohydrates.

Fig bars. These remain old standbys because riders find them easy to eat and agreeable to the stomach. And they have virtually no fat. Two bars provide about 140 calories, 32 grams of carbohydrate (91 percent), 2 grams of protein, and 2 grams of fat (13 percent).

Fruit. You may not expect convenience stores to carry the natural stuff. Most do, but prices tend to be higher than in conventional grocery stores. When available and affordable, almost any fruit is great for a carb refuel with lots of vitamins, minerals, and fiber, too. A banana has about 100 calories of energy, an apple about 80, and an orange about 60. None contain significant amounts of fat or protein.

Corn nuts. Some cyclists say that they crave salt rather than sugar when their energy runs low. If this includes you, do yourself a favor: Skip the potato chips, which are about 58 percent fat. A 2-ounce serving of Corn Nuts will satisfy your salty desires and deliver about 20 grams of carbohydrate (62 percent) in 130 calories, 2 grams of protein, and 4 grams of fat (28 percent).

Pretzels. These are another alternative to chips. But great-tasting pretzels, such as Keebler's Butter Braids, can be difficult to find in single-serving bags. If you go for the larger size, keep in mind that 2 ounces gives you 220 calories, 44 grams of carbohydrate (80 percent), 6 grams of protein, and 2 grams of fat (8 percent).

V8 juice. Sure, Mom said eat your vegetables, but V8 lets you drink them. This beverage is primarily tomato juice mixed with seven other veggies. It contains more vitamins and minerals than many sports drinks and has significant amounts of two antioxidants (nutrients that help your body eliminate destructive free radicals). Slam back a V8, and you get 100 percent of the Daily Value for vitamin C and 70 percent for vitamin A. A 12-ounce serving contains 70 calories, 15 grams of carbohydrate (86 percent), 3 grams of protein, and no fat.

Marshmallow munchies. Hello, sugar high! Most marshmallow treats are blended with crisped rice, another carbohydrate powerhouse. A typical 57-gram bar (about 2 ounces) contains 220 calories, 43 grams of carbohydrate (78 percent), 2 grams of protein, and 5 grams of fat (20 percent).

Hostess brownies. Some cyclists still swear by Twinkies (not a bad cycling food with 286 calories in a 2-ounce package), but we always opt for Hostess's low-fat brownies instead. These gooey chocolate treats are good enough to fool even die-hard fans of full-fat brownies. Nutrient content is 140 calories, 29 grams of carbohydrate (83 percent), 2 grams of protein, and just under 3 grams of fat (19 percent).

Milky Way Lite candy bar. If you must indulge a junk-food fix or perish, reach for a Milky Way Lite. It's so yummy that you'll never know it's lower in fat than the original. A 1.5-ounce bar provides 160 calories, 33 grams of carbohydrate (83 percent), 2 grams of protein, and 5 grams of fat (28 percent). That's about half the fat of most candy bars.

FAST-FOOD RESTAURANTS

These places are a fixture in our lives and on the landscape because they offer two qualities sacred to Americans—speed and convenience. Fortunately, you needn't sabotage your hard-earned health when supping at these American icons on the way to, from, or even during a ride.

It's true that a moment of weakness with a double cheeseburger and fries can supply you with several day's worth of fat. But despite what the nutrition cops say, not all fast food is trash food. Most of the major franchises also offer low-fat items on their menus.

Here are 13 fast-food choices. Each falls within the guidelines for a healthful cycling diet, with fat limited to under 30 percent of total calories.

McDonald's apple bran muffin. Coupled with a 6-ounce glass of orange juice (80 calories, no fat), this is an excellent alternative to the Egg McMuffin, which has 280 calories and 11 grams of fat (35 percent). The no-fat muffin has 180 calories, 40 grams of carbohydrate, 5 grams of protein, and no fat. Long ride ahead? Buy a carton of skim milk and pour it into a bowl of McDonald's Wheaties (1 gram of fat) or Cheerios (same).

Hardee's pancakes. Skip the margarine and top this dish with jam. Three pancakes have 280 calories, 56 grams of carbohydrate, 8 grams of protein, and less than 1 gram of fat (less than 3 percent).

Dunkin' Donuts's cinnamon 'n' raisin bagel. Unlike even the plain cake doughnut, which has a whopping 262 calories and 18 grams of fat (61 percent), a bagel will rev you up without devastating your diet. One bagel has 250 calories, 49 grams of carbohydrate, 8 grams of protein, and 2 grams of fat (7 percent).

Arby's Light Roast Turkey Deluxe. This is the top-rated sandwich on this list. Combine it with a garden salad and orange juice for a meal that barely totals 10 grams of fat. The sandwich has 249 calories, 33 grams of carbohydrate, 19 grams of protein, and 4 grams of fat (14 percent).

Hardee's grilled chicken sandwich. Despite its high sodium content, this sandwich has one-third the fat of a typical fried chicken sandwich. But ask for it mayo-free or scrape off the calorie-rich dressing yourself to cut the fat in half. As sold, the sandwich has 310 calories, 34 grams of carbohydrate, 24 grams of protein, and 9 grams of fat (26 percent). (McDonald's grilled chicken sandwich is comparable. Served with lettuce and tomato only, it has 250 calories, 33 grams of carbohydrate, 24 grams of protein, and 3 grams of fat.)

Long John Silver's baked fish with paprika. This two-piece "light portion" of baked fish fillet includes rice pilaf and a small salad, and is one of the best-rated fast-food meals. It includes 300 calories, 45 grams of carbohydrate, 24 grams of protein, and 2 grams of fat (6 percent). Even Long John's fries are better than everyone else's—a small order totals 170 calories with 6 grams of fat (32 percent), and it has no added salt.

KFC's mashed potatoes and gravy and corn-on-the-cob. It's hard to recommend KFC with so many of its two-piece dinners containing an artery-clogging 50 or more grams of fat. But the potatoes and gravy aren't bad. Combine two orders of potatoes and gravy for 142 calories with 24 grams of carbohydrate, 4 grams of protein, and 4 grams of fat (25 percent) with an order of corn on the cob—176 calories, 32 grams of carbohydrate, 5 grams of protein, and 3 grams of fat (15 percent).

Burger King's broiled chicken sandwich. When it comes to low-fat nutrition, Burger King's flame-broiled chunk chicken patty sandwich is the company's only saving grace. It contains 267 calories, 28 grams of carbohydrate, 22 grams of protein, and 8 grams of fat (27 percent). But don't confuse it with the company's standard chicken sandwich, which packs an incredible 40 grams of fat.

McDonald's chunky chicken salad with light vinaigrette dressing. You can't go wrong with this green plate. In fact, order two if you're hungry. The unadulterated salad has 198 calories, 7 grams of carbohydrate, 25 grams of protein, and 4 grams of fat (18 percent). Lite Vinaigrette dressing adds only 48 calories and 2 grams of fat.

Subway's 6-inch turkey sub. The commonly ordered 12-inch sub is filling but fattening. Instead, go for the 6-inch version, skip the mayo and cheese, and add a large garden salad. The sandwich has 322 calories, 41 grams of carbohydrate, 21 grams of protein, and 2 grams of fat (6 percent)—10 grams of fat with mayo and cheese. The salad has 26 calories, 10 grams of carbohydrate, 2 grams of protein, and no fat.

Taco Bell's soft chicken taco without cheese. Taco Bell's offerings smell seductively yummy but are among the most fattening. On the plus side, the Bell is good about customizing orders and has removed the lard from its beans. Ordering the Soft Chicken Taco without cheese cuts the fat in half. (Ask them to hold the cheese on a side order of pinto beans and you'll eliminate another 7 grams of fat.) The taco has 213 calories, 19 grams of carbohydrate, 14 grams of protein, and 4 grams of fat (17 percent) without cheese (10 grams with it). Pinto beans and cheese have 190 calories, 19 grams of carbohydrate, 9 grams of protein, and 9 grams of fat.

Wendy's baked potato. A carb-booster and glycogen-recharger, Wendy's plain baked potato is low-fat and sodium-free. One 9-ounce potato has 270 calories, 67 grams of carbohydrate, 8 grams of protein, and less than 1 gram of fat (less than 3 percent). Order a one-trip-through side salad from the salad bar and load up on fresh vegetables, sliced mushrooms, onions, tomatoes, peas, shredded carrots, and broccoli. Skip the butter, sour cream, bacon bits, seeds, and cheese.

Wendy's chili. Beef-eaters will be glad to know that there is a meaty meal they can eat that doesn't bust the 30 percent fat barrier. A 9-ounce bowl of this chili has 220 calories, 23 grams of carbohydrate, 21 grams of protein, and 7 grams of fat (28 percent). It's especially good combined with a spud.

As you can see, it is possible to have it your way—the low-fat way. Realize, though, that the menus at fast-food places change almost as fast as your order is ready. Some of the dishes above may become obsolete while healthful new items take their places. Choose carefully. Remember that you can keep the fat content reasonable on many items simply by rejecting cheese, dressing, mayo, sour cream, and butter.

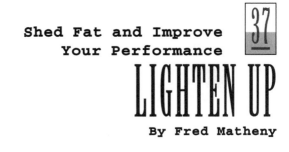

LIGHTEN UP

By Fred Matheny

Road cycling is famous for riders who spare no expense to lighten their bikes while packing 10 extra pounds inside their jerseys. It's always helpful to save weight, but the place to start is on your body. Trimming excess fat will help your performance as it improves your power-to-weight ratio, and it's good for overall health and appearance, too.

On the other hand, nutritional excesses and cycling seem to go together. Many riders have ridden for hours, then rewarded their efforts with a fat-laden meal at a Mexican restaurant.

The good news is that you don't have to forgo your favorite foods in order to lose weight. Here are four important pointers for unpacking the extra baggage, followed by real-life tips from two riders who did.

Rely on more than diets. Sure, you lose weight when you cut calories, but all of the lost poundage isn't fat. A significant percentage—up to 30 percent—is muscle tissue. Dieters often end up thinner but slower and weaker. As pioneering diet writer Covert Bailey argues, "When someone says that they lost 20 pounds, the key question is: 20 pounds of what?" Some dieters end up weighing less but having a higher percentage of body fat. And don't forget that muscle burns calories. The more muscle volume you have, the more calories you consume. If you lose muscle, you gain fat faster when you return to pre-diet eating habits.

Ride, ride, ride. The average road cyclist consumes about 40 calories per mile. (See "Calculating Cycling Calories" on page 156 to see how many calories you burn.) At a relatively sedate 15 miles per hour, this means a weekly time commitment of 10 hours on the bike can burn a whopping 6,000 calories. A weekend century ride requires

CALCULATING CYCLING CALORIES

How many calories does cycling burn? This is one of the questions that riders ask most, but there is no precise answer. It depends on many factors: body size, type of bike, pace, terrain, and wind conditions, to name a few. It is known, however, that the energy used in cycling increases dramatically with speed because of the increase in wind resistance.

The adjoining chart shows calorie consumption estimates for different body weights and speeds. These numbers were developed by physiologist James Hagberg, Ph.D. Simply choose your average speed and multiply your weight by the coefficient for that speed and you'll have a close approximation of the calories you burn per minute.

Going uphill adds to this energy cost. It's estimated that 22 extra calories are burned for every 100 feet of elevation gained, so factor this in. (This value is for a cyclist and bike weighing a total of 176 pounds.) Coasting downhill burns no extra calories, of course, but the combination of going up and down always uses more energy than riding on flat ground.

Average Speed (mph)	Coefficient (cal./lb./min.)
8	0.0295
10	0.0355
12	0.0426
14	0.0512
15	0.0561
16	0.0615
17	0.0675
18	0.0740
19	0.0811
20	0.0891
21	0.0975
23	0.1173
25	0.1411

about 4,000 calories, quite a lot when you consider that you lose a pound of body fat for every 3,200 calories you burn. Thanks to the non-weight-bearing nature of cycling, almost no one is too heavy to ride. Even obese people can do significant miles without suffering the joint problems they might experience from running or walking.

Boost the carbs, trim the fat. Your problem may not be how much you eat but the nutritional balance among carbohydrate, fat, and protein. The diet that is proven best for high-level endurance performance—60 to 70 percent carbohydrate with less than 30 percent fat, also works for weight loss. It usually isn't necessary to make radical adjustments to achieve these percentages. Small changes work best. For instance, substitute light margarine for high-fat margarine on your toast. Don't eat a whole bowl of chili with meat—fill half the bowl with brown rice, then ladle a small amount of chili on top. Substitute bagels for muffins, nonfat yogurt for sour cream, and fruit for sweets.

Keep your upper body fit. Because cycling is primarily a leg sport, riders can lose muscle volume in their upper bodies and look flabby. Even pro mountain bikers, who use their arms and shoulders more than road riders, often must do weight work to keep their top half buffed. This is important, remember, because if you lose muscle, you don't burn as many calories. The solution is year-round resistance training. But this doesn't mean hours in the weight room. As little as 20 minutes twice a week during the cycling season, and 30 minutes two or three times weekly during the winter, will maintain and even increase your muscle mass. (For more information on weight training, see chapter 30.)

LIVING PROOF

To show how well this approach works, two riders, both in their forties and who used cycling to trim excess pounds, offer their advice. If you want to do the same, these examples will help you design a program that works for you, too.

Ralph Phillips

The owner of Fairwheel Bikes in Tucson, Arizona, regularly trains with (and keeps up with) talented cyclists half his age. Riding with Phillips, you would never guess that when he was a sophomore in high school, he was 5-foot-1 and weighed 185 pounds. Now he's 5-foot-8 and 135. He can't tell you how to grow 7 inches, but he does have some insights on losing weight.

Go long and easy. "Take a long, slow ride once a week, especially in the early season," says Phillips. "I often go for 6 hours, but I don't go fast and beat my brains out. Long rides burn a lot of fat and give you a good base for later in the season."

Recharge properly. Recovery matters. "Refuel with plenty of carbohydrate. Don't think that you'll lose weight faster if you don't eat. You'll just get weak and feel terrible the next day," notes Phillips. "Also, be sure to take recovery rides. Our training rides on Wednesdays, Fridays, and Sundays are slow and easy. I tell the racers that I'll shoot 'em if they go fast. And don't forget that it's a long season, especially in warm-weather climates. We ride year-round in Tucson, so everyone burns out in July and needs some physical and mental time off the bike."

Fill up on water. There's that word again. You can't ride enough in summer heat to lose weight unless you hydrate. "In this climate we don't need to think too much about drinking plenty of water—if you don't, you won't last long," says Phillips. "Be sure that you always start with at least two full bottles. We plan our rides so we can stop at drinking fountains or convenience stores along the way and tank up."

Sherri Black

A secretary at a community college in upstate New York, Black is the weight-loss comeback kid. In 1979, she won a cycling bronze medal in the Empire State Games, a mini-Olympics for New York residents. Then came marriage, a business, two children—and 65 unwanted pounds. In 1993, divorced and a single mother, Black decided to lose weight and return to racing. Two years later, she won the 10-mile time trial and the Masters 45-to-54 road race at the Empire State Games. Here is what she learned.

Short rides can still do the trick. "I get home from work at 4:00 P.M. and have to pick up a child at day care by 5:30. So I don't have much time to train," Black explains. "But even 40 minutes of cycling can help you lose weight if you go hard. You could ride indoors, but that doesn't work for me. I need to get outside even if it's just for a walk."

Eat in moderation. "I try to cut fat from my diet and eat lots of vegetables. In fact, I have my own garden. But I don't go overboard. Moderation is important," says Black. "I have a sweet tooth so I eat candy sometimes, and dessert. If you always deprive yourself, you might binge. Eating low-calorie veggies and carbohydrate instead of fat lets me eat a lot of food. That's one reason that I like to ride—I can eat a lot."

Increase your pep. Have faith that as you drop weight, you will gain more pep. "Cycling raises your energy level. Once you get used to the idea of riding, it gets easier to get out there. It's a reward in itself and really makes me feel rejuvenated. I come back feeling like a new person. Noncyclists don't have the energy levels we do," says Black.

Medical Concerns

OVERTRAINING

By Geoff Drake

Cycling, it's been said, is a sport for tough guys, and the toughest never utter the word *overtrained*. For them, nagging fatigue is a phenomenon of the mind and not the legs, and the solution is simple: Ride more to get stronger.

Ann Snyder, Ph.D., met a bunch of these tough guys and decided to find out how stalwart they really are. For two weeks she subjected them to more than 10 hours of interval training per week, plus races on weekends. One rider couldn't sustain the load, dropping from the study after six days. Seven of them survived. By the end, only one was able to finish a race.

The findings? Bike riders are indeed tough. "Cyclists are crazy," says Dr. Snyder with a mixture of awe and fascination. "You can get them to do anything."

Aside from this simple summation, she found a few more concrete things as well. All the subjects displayed a downturn in performance, as indicated by time trial and power output tests. Sleeping heart rate increased, while maximum heart rate declined. Also, subjective responses to a questionnaire showed a deterioration in their "general state of well-being."

But most interesting, after a two-week rest period in which the training load was roughly halved, performance reached its former level or improved. This points out one of the central dilemmas of training: We know that hard work makes us faster, but how much is too much? And how long does it take to recover and experience this rebound effect?

OVERREACHING

Exercise physiologists are fond of making a distinction between over-training, which is debilitating and long-term (lasting weeks or months), and overreaching, which is what we feel at the end of a particularly hard week of riding. With adequate recovery overreaching will make us faster and stronger. Unfortunately, there is no distinct border between the two conditions. And either way, it's dangerous country to be in.

Dr. Snyder, director of the exercise physiology lab at the University of Wisconsin in Milwaukee, found this out in no uncertain terms while conducting her research. Although a few of her hardy bunch improved under the intense regimen, all showed physiological danger signs. In fact, for anyone who considers overtraining to be a figment of the imagination, the study debunked that concept with a fusillade of data, including the following:

Max VO$_2$. This measure of the body's ability to deliver oxygen to working muscles declined significantly, reaching its lowest point at the end of the intense training period.

Sleeping heart rate. Increased about five beats per minute after the hard period.

Maximum heart rate. Declined about seven beats per minute. In a race this could translate to a slower time.

Subjective evaluation. Riders were asked such questions as, "Would you like to skip training?" or "Do you feel as if you're not recovered?" Not surprisingly, there was a distinct lack of enthusiasm during the study. The moping was most pronounced the week after the intense training, during the rest period.

But what's even more important, two performance markers also slipped.

Time trials. Riders raced an 8.5-kilometer course once per week. Performance slowed significantly, an average of 41 seconds in the week after intense training. Also, riders could not attain the same heart rate that they did in the first time trial when they were fresh.

Maximum power output. Cyclists performed a weekly ergometer test in which the load increased by 50 watts every 5 minutes until exhaustion. The result? Power output declined an average of 26 watts after the intensive training.

Of all Dr. Snyder's measurements, the only ones that didn't change were weight and body fat percentage.

Despite the obvious risks, let's say that you decide to embark on a similar period of intense training, or overreaching. How long must you rest before you can reap the benefits? Dr. Snyder's study supplied some answers here, too. The two key performance variables (time trials and maximum power output) continued to improve throughout the two-week recovery period. In other words, the typical two days of tapering before an important event may not be enough. Although the study ended after two weeks of recovery, the findings suggest that performance may have continued to improve with even more rest.

Who is prone to these dangers? Turns out that in the land of over-training, cyclists occupy a prominent spot. In fact, few other athletes seem capable of inducing such a bone-deep weariness. According to Dr. Snyder, this may be due to the concentrated way that cycling stresses the body. "Cyclists' muscles could become overtrained sooner because they're using mainly the quadriceps," she says. "Runners use more muscle mass. With cyclists, if the quads are tired, the rider will be tired."

Also, it may come as a surprise that you needn't undergo a titanic training load to be overtrained. In fact, working folks, with sporadic and relatively light riding schedules, may be most likely to experience such problems, according to a study that reviewed overtraining. "Less experienced athletes and those who train themselves may be particularly prone," the report says, because they either emulate the programs of elite riders or fail to recognize the symptoms of overtraining. In other words, it's all relative. Your 100-mile weeks may be a postrace cooldown for Lance Armstrong, but if you only rode 20 miles in the previous week, your body could show all the symptoms of over-training.

WARNING SIGNS

How do you guard against the perils of overtraining? While most riders don't have access to the sophisticated measuring methods used by exercise physiologists, a few key things can be monitored.

Resting heart rate. Dr. Snyder's study showed a significant increase in sleeping heart rate, but not much change in resting pulse first thing in the morning, the traditional measurement. Another study in which runners doubled their training mileage, however, showed a morning increase of about 10 beats per minute, and most cycling coaches emphasize this measurement. Record your pulse upon waking under the same conditions each day, and beware of significant increases.

Disposition. While this may seem the vaguest possible index, it may be one of the most reliable. In one 10-year study involving swimmers, measurements of such things as anger, depression, and vigor worsened markedly when training loads were doubled. When every pothole seems like a personal insult, beware.

Time trial performance. Dr. Snyder recommends doing a short time trial in similar conditions every other week while building for a big event. "I wouldn't worry about a time that's 5 seconds slower," she says. "But if you're off by a minute, it could be due to overtraining."

Time trial heart rate. A drop of 10 beats per minute or so in your average heart rate can indicate overtraining. Some heart-rate monitors calculate average beats per minute for you. If yours doesn't, note the highest heart rate attained during the time trial. Should this begin declining, overtraining could be the reason.

The rebound effect. The key is whether your regimen enables you to go faster, or longer, in your targeted events. If after a period of intense training, you show no performance benefit, then you may not have rested enough. Moreover, if you continue to ride hard in the face of this evidence, you may end up overtrained.

"Overreaching could be part of your normal training cycle," says Dr. Snyder. "If you rest for a few days, you'll recover. But with overtraining it could require a month or two. The bottom line is that both will lead to detriments in performance unless you take days off."

Rest. It could be the toughest training choice you'll ever make.

Banish Them Forever

SADDLE SORES

By Fred Matheny

The worst saddle sore I ever had—a swollen, festering volcano of a boil—sprouted two days before the district time trial championship. Riding that day was like being impaled on the business end of a white-hot 60-penny spike. The all-purpose term *saddle sore*, however, includes not only boils but also chafing, bruises, and ulcerated skin.

Crotch carbuncles have transformed pleasant rides into medieval torture ever since the days of wool shorts and leather chamois. Old-time racers thus afflicted would line their shorts with thin pieces of raw steak to help minimize the pain. Left untreated, saddle sores can become infected and require extended time off the bike. But you don't have to suffer perineal misery (or ruin a good sirloin) if you practice a few simple preventive measures.

Pad your bottom. Traditional cycling shorts with a padded, synthetic insert (called a chamois) are your best defense against saddle sores. The chamois used to be made of slow-drying leather. Several washings robbed it of natural oils and made perching on its crinkly folds as comfortable as sitting on a tortilla chip. Modern synthetics are softer on the skin than traditional leather, and they also wick away the moisture that can hasten the formation of sores—something their animal-base ancestors could not do.

Well-made shorts have a chamois designed so that the seams don't rub you raw. You may have to try several brands before you find something compatible with your anatomy. If you prefer loose-fitting shorts that look like the ones hikers wear, they should still have a sewn-in liner with a padded insert. Most women do best with a one-piece chamois or one that's formed by a "baseball" cut that avoids seams on the midline.

Avoid the rookie mistake of wearing underwear beneath cycling shorts. This defeats the idea of special-purpose cycling shorts. Nothing should come between your skin and the chamois except, perhaps, some lubrication.

Eliminate friction. Because irritation is a major cause of saddle sores, lubricate "any usual area of friction," before you ride, says Andrew Pruitt, Ed.D., chief medical officer for the U.S. Cycling Federation and director of Table Mesa Sports and Rehabilitation in Boulder, Colorado. "Use something that isn't readily water-soluble, such as petroleum jelly, so it will be there at the end of the ride. Sweat and rain dissolve some commercial chamois creams."

Wash up. The nasty bacteria that cause boils love hot, moist environments—and nothing is quite as steamy as your hardworking buns, encased in tight-fitting cycling shorts on a hot summer day. Use soap and water or rubbing alcohol on a washcloth to thoroughly cleanse your crotch before each ride. Afterward, wash carefully in the shower and towel dry. Apply alcohol to disinfect your skin again, unless it has become raw or broken.

Washing is especially important if you applied a greasy lubricant. "You have to cleanse your skin carefully (after using petroleum jelly or anti-friction creams) to avoid clogged pores," says Dr. Pruitt. "Also, wash your shorts thoroughly after every ride to remove the grease. It's no problem in a washing machine, but can be more difficult on a trip doing laundry by hand in the sink."

Always wear clean cycling shorts for each ride, even on a tour or bike camping trip where scrubbing them may be difficult. "Soiled shorts have more bacteria, and they don't breathe as well as freshly laundered ones," cautions Arnie Baker, M.D., a *Bicycling* magazine fitness advisory board member and author of *Smart Cycling*. And don't walk around after a ride with a clammy chamois stuck to your skin. Wash up and change into loose shorts that allow the air to circulate. To keep your crotch dry for 6 to 8 hours at a time, sleep in the buff.

Medicate yourself. If you are prone to saddle sores, apply a topical antibiotic gel such as erythromycin after every ride, recommends *Bicycling* fitness advisory board member Bernard Burton, M.D.

On a transcontinental ride I smeared on the prescription brand Emgel each day. Result? Not one saddle sore despite averaging 140 miles a day for three weeks on America's bumpy backroads.

If you develop a raw area from friction, Dr. Burton recommends an over-the-counter product called Bag Balm, "developed to soothe a milk cow's irritated teats." Look for it at your pharmacy or animal supply store and cow those saddle sores into submission. "Bag Balm applied to irritated areas after your shower will usually clear up the problem overnight," he says.

Some riders treat hot spots with topical steroid ointment, but Dr. Burton cautions against it. He says that such ointments can cause thinning of the skin and the possibility of an acnelike eruption.

Level your seat. Poor position on the bike can cause a bumper crop of sores. According to Dr. Pruitt, "If your saddle is too high, you will rock back and forth across it, irritating and breaching the skin." The same is true of saddles that aren't level. Tilted up, the nose rubs directly on the front of the pubic area. Tilt it down more than a degree or two, and you'll continually slide forward, then push yourself back. The resulting friction can rub you raw. If you suspect that poor position may be the culprit, check yours with the guidelines in chapter 1.

Give it a rest. You don't want to stop riding, but getting the pressure off a budding sore for a couple of days may save you a week or more on the disabled list by preventing it from becoming infected. Count Eddy Merckx and Sean Kelly among the many pro stars who had to abandon races because minor eruptions grew into major medical problems. "Continuing to ride on an abscess," cautions Dr. Burton, "could result in multiple infections, scarring, and the tendency for more of these lesions to develop, often without additional trauma."

Take a bath. "Soak in a comfortably hot bathtub three times a day for 15 minutes to allow boils to come to the surface and drain," says Dr. Baker. "Hot water increases blood circulation, allowing more of the body's healing factors access to the afflicted area."

Suspend the ride. According to Dr. Burton, "Riding a road bike with rear suspension eliminates about 90 percent of saddle sores. Suspension seatposts also help. Suspension reduces friction because you stay connected to the seat on rough pavement rather than bouncing up and down. Fully suspended mountain bikes have the same effect." As of 1997, Softride was the main company producing rear-suspended road bikes. Suspension seatposts can be retrofit to any conventional bike.

Okay, you have tried all the above but still sprouted a saddle sore—

and the tour that you have trained for all season starts tomorrow. What to do?

Dr. Pruitt, who often tends to U.S. national team riders at international races, suggests applying a topical lidocaine ointment to numb the sore, then cushioning it with a nonstick, moist burn pad. Visit a drugstore for these products.

In many cases, however, riding is out of the question. Some boils must be lanced and the unfortunate rider given a course of antibiotics. Sometimes even more heroic measures are required. "When I had bad saddle sores, I continued training," reveals Dr. Baker, a several-time masters national champion. "I did hill sprints and intervals—all off the saddle and off my sores."

NUMBNESS

By the Editors of *Bicycling* Magazine

For as long as cycling has existed, riders have complained about body parts falling asleep. A bike exerts pressure on each part of the anatomy it touches, compressing nerves and blood vessels. It doesn't take long for tingling and discomfort to begin. Unless the pressure is relieved, numbness follows. Continued episodes can even cause long-term disability.

In this chapter medical experts who are experienced with cycling provide answers to some of the typical complaints voiced by cyclists. Use this information to remedy problems you may encounter. Even better, use it to avoid them altogether.

Q. How can I prevent my fingers from going numb?

A. Numb fingers are caused by compression of the ulnar nerve, which runs from the neck through the forearm to the ring and little fingers. To prevent this compression, use a firm-but-relaxed grip on the handlebar and change hand position frequently. Padded cycling gloves and cork handlebar tape also help.

In addition, make sure that your bar, top tube, and stem are properly sized. If correct, your view of the front hub will be obscured by the handlebar when you're sitting comfortably with your hands on the brake hoods. Many road cyclists have found relief from numb fingers by using a bolt-on aero bar. Its elbow rests relieve ulnar nerve pressure entirely.

If numbness persists, additional treatment can include icing, ultrasound, or anti-inflammatory medication. In severe cases surgical decompression of the nerve might be necessary.

—Alan Bragman, D.C.

Q. Is it true that long-term pressure or jarring of the wrists during cycling can cause carpal tunnel syndrome?

A. The median nerve, which passes through the carpal tunnel, affects sensation of the thumb, the next two fingers, and half of the ring finger. Carpal tunnel syndrome is usually associated with excessive repetitive motion or vibration of the wrist. Ultramarathon riders used to have such problems before aero bars. Mountain bikers may get symptoms because of the jarring on rough terrain. It is unusual in roadies or track riders, though.

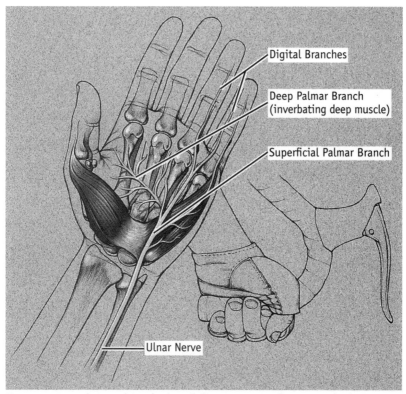

Nerve compression against the handlebar can cause fingers to tingle or become numb.

Ulnar neuropathy—sometimes called cyclist's palsy—is more common to the sport. The ulnar nerve affects sensation of the pinkie and half the ring finger. Pressure on the palm below these fingers can cause pain or numbness. Use the remedies described in the first answer. The best wrist position for general riding is a relaxed one in a neutral position. Avoid excessive tension or bending.

—Arnie Baker, M.D.

Q. What can I do about numbness and pain in my feet, particularly on long rides?

A. Numb toes result from lack of blood flow caused by several factors. The sensation that results is often confused with one of heat. Overly tight shoes or toe straps are common culprits. During a ride your feet swell, so loosen your shoe closures or straps. When buying cycling shoes, wear the same socks you use when riding and make sure there is room to wiggle your toes.

Constant pressure on the ball of the foot can also numb your toes. This compresses nerves and prevents blood from reaching the front of the foot. Foam insoles can help reduce this problem, but arch supports or orthotics are even more effective. They redistribute the pressure to a wider area of the foot, namely the arch and heel.

Another cause can be nerve irritation. Two sets of nerves reach the toes. One runs along the bottom of the foot, the other across the top. The nerves on the top are close to the skin and easily irritated. A clipless pedal system, which by nature produces less stress here than toe straps, isn't as likely to irritate these nerves. Another option is to select a shoe with a soft upper area or modify your present shoes with foam padding.

The nerves on the bottom of the foot run between the foot bones and into the toes. They can become irritated when pinched between the bones. In this case wider shoes are often a solution. This irritation can also be caused by your position on the pedal. Long-distance cyclists sometimes find it helpful to move their cleats rearward about an inch.

Windchill contributes, too. It causes the body to redirect blood from its extremities to its core. So even if your feet are protected by shoe covers or booties in winter, a chilly torso is still likely to result in numb toes.

—Douglas Ehrenberg, D.P.M.

Q. Should a male cyclist be concerned because his penis occasionally goes numb while riding?

A. Yes. Numbness is caused by the saddle's compression of the perineum. This is the area of the crotch that houses the nerves and blood vessels that feed the penis. Long-term compression may result in blood flow so reduced that the cyclist becomes impotent (unable to gain or retain an erection sufficient for intercourse), says Boston urologist Irwin Goldstein, M.D., one the country's premier impotency experts. He says that he has reason to believe that this cycling condition has caused several of his patients to lose their sexual function.

It helps to understand the male plumbing. The penis is a hydraulic system. During sexual stimulation its twin chambers fill with blood until it's firm and erect. After stimulation ends or if there is ejaculation, the blood leaves and the penis softens again. The nerve impulse for this increased blood flow, and the flow itself, travel through the perineum. This is located between your "sit bones." To better understand the geography, squat and sit on a low step or curb. You will feel your weight being supported by the two large bones of your pelvis, as evolution intended. But when you are on a bicycle seat, your weight is concentrated between these bones, directly on the perineum.

"Fifty percent of the penis is actually inside the body," Dr. Goldstein explains. "When you sit on a bicycle seat, you're putting your entire body weight on the artery that supplies the penis." Of equal concern to Dr. Goldstein are accidents that cause impacts against the top tube or stem, causing injuries that leave a male unable to function sexually.

"I cannot say that sitting on a bicycle seat causes impotence," Dr. Goldstein explains, "but I can go on record with supporting data to show that sitting on a bicycle seat compresses the artery. It's intuitive that if you took a straw and sat on it, however, a certain percentage of the time the straw would jump back and be a circular structure. But if you keep doing this, at some point the straw is going to take on sort of an oval shape (or flatten). I can't prove that long-term compression causes impotency, but I kind of think that it does in a very small percentage of cases."

To make sure you're not so unlucky, follow these 10 tips to reduce short-term numbness and long-term risk.

1. Level your saddle. Or point the nose a degree or two downward to ease the pressure on your crotch.

2. Lower your saddle. Your knees should be slightly bent when your feet are at the bottom of each pedal stroke. This will prevent rocking across the saddle and will let your legs support more of your weight.

3. Be wary of aero bars. For all their advantages, they encourage you to ride on the saddle's nose for long periods, putting excessive pressure on your crotch.

4. Try a different saddle. There are dozens of models. Find one wide enough to support your weight on your sit bones instead of your perineum.

5. Stand to pedal every 10 minutes. This will open your blood vessels and return maximum circulation to your penis. Do this whether riding outdoors or in.

6. Use your legs as shock absorbers. Level the pedals and rise out of the saddle for railroad tracks, patched pavement, washboard ripples, or anything else that can jolt your crotch.

7. Check your bike size. When straddling your road bike, there should be at least 2 inches between your crotch and the top tube. This is a safety margin to reduce the risk of an impact injury. Also consider padding the top tube with pipe insulation like on a BMX bike.

8. Ride shorter distances. You don't need to pedal 50 miles to get a good workout. Half this distance will do it if you stress quality over quantity.

9. Cross-train. Any sport, when taken to the extreme, can have injurious overuse effects. If you are seeking weight control and fitness, try activities that add enjoyment and subtract saddle time.

10. Heed numbness. If you lose sensation in your penis while riding, it is a sure sign that you are pinching the nerves and arteries of the perineum. Get out of the saddle more frequently as you head for home. (For more information on penile numbness, see chapter 42.)

—Joe Kita

Q. What can be done about neck and back pain on longer rides?

A. Cycling-related strains like these are often associated with the physical stress of being on the bike for long periods. Riding position is often a key factor. Cyclists lacking flexibility may find an aerodynamic, bent-over posture uncomfortable. Stretching and close attention to position (see chapter 1) should help.

These pains may also arise from muscle tension due to stress, anxiety, depression, fatigue, or poor posture. Jarring from rough roads also can contribute.

If pain occurs only on longer rides, allow for a gradual increase in endurance. Do not boost mileage more than 10 percent per week. Consciously relax your upper body—back, shoulders, and neck—every few minutes. Change hand positions often, which will change neck and back angle. Stretch on the bike by standing, coasting, moving your hips forward, and arching your back. Look around to keep your neck loose. Don't focus only on the pavement directly in front of you with your head locked in position.

If your problem is from craning your neck to see, ride with a more upright posture. Put your hands on the brake hoods or handlebar top. If this doesn't do it, consider a higher and/or shorter stem. If your reach is still too long, you may have to switch to a bike with a shorter top tube.

If road shock is the culprit, consider a gel-padded saddle or even a suspension seatpost. Level your crankarms when going over bumps so you can soften them with bent knees.

Strengthening your muscles may help, but don't try it while you are still sore or tight. Back extensions and crunches condition your lower back. For your neck try isometric exercises by using your hand to resist the up-and-down and side-to-side motion of your head.

Anti-inflammatory pain medicines such as ibuprofen, aspirin, or naproxen are often useful. Chiropractic manipulation helps some people overcome pain. Surgery is usually the last-resort treatment. A surgical emergency may exist if the nerves being pinched in the neck interfere with muscle sensation or power elsewhere in the body.

Finally, a bulge or herniation of an intervertebral disk may cause pain that travels to the arms. Pain in the front of the neck or jaw, especially if associated with chest discomfort, may be due to heart problems. If any of these symptoms appear, see a physician.

—Arnie Baker, M.D.

Preserving These Tricky Joints

KNEES

By Fred Matheny

Ugly medical terms are associated with knees and bikes, words that sound like trouble when you say them. Chondromalacia, patellar tendinitis, medial synovial plica syndrome, iliotibial band syndrome—a medical rogues' gallery of pain and misery.

Does this mean that bike riding is hard on knees? Far from it. In fact, when these injuries are mentioned, cycling's connection to most of them is as the rehabilitation of choice. Physical therapists know that when you can't run, walk, or hobble, you can often pedal.

"Injured or surgically repaired knees want movement, and you want movement," says Andrew Pruitt, Ed.D., chief medical officer for the U.S. Cycling Federation and director of Table Mesa Sports Medicine and Rehabilitation in Boulder, Colorado. "These things come together on the bike."

Still, knee injuries are occasionally a fact of cycling life. "The cycling knee is unique," explains Dr. Pruitt, "due to the number of revolutions it makes." At an average cadence of 90 revolutions per minute, a rider cranks out 5,400 strokes each hour or about 1.5 million in a 5,000-mile year. That's a lot of potential wear and tear on cartilage, ligaments, and tendons.

Repetition isn't the only villain. The knee is anything but a simple joint that pumps up and down in a linear, pistonlike motion. Instead, Dr. Pruitt says, "the knee rolls, glides, and rotates" in several planes during each pedal stroke. The cycling leg is anchored at the bottom by the foot, which is attached to the pedal with a rigid shoe. At the other end is the massive bone and ligament edifice of the hip joint. The knee moves between these fixed points, and if this isn't accommodated by correct position on the bike and proper placement of the foot on the pedal, bad things happen.

Road cycling, interestingly enough, is said to be more hazardous to knees than mountain biking. It sounds counterintuitive; mountain biking involves the sort of high-torque, low-revolution-per-minute grinding that knee experts have warned against for years. Even so, Dr. Pruitt argues, "Road riding is more dangerous because of all the repetitive pedal strokes in one position." Off road you're all over the bike, but what looks ugly and inelegant has protective value.

So how do you safeguard your precious knees so that 10 to 20 million pedal strokes down the road they will still be going strong? The key is knowing what to do and what to avoid—on the bike or off.

GOOD FORM

First, perfect your position. Problems aren't limited to neophytes. Even experienced riders make mistakes when setting up a new bike. And position sometimes seems to be a fashion statement—low and to the rear one year, forward and high the next. Knees don't like the vagaries of style. They prefer consistency.

Dr. Pruitt, in his work with the U.S. national cycling team, has pioneered the "dynamic bike fit." This means he fits the bike to a rider who is pedaling rather than stationary. With his computerized system he can quantify exactly what the knees are doing at different points in the pedal stroke.

Lacking such wizardry, static measurements can approximate your ideal position. For saddle height, stand shoeless with your feet shoulder-width apart and have someone measure your inseam, from the floor to your crotch; multiply the result by 0.883. The result is your seat height from the top of the saddle to the middle of the bottom bracket axle measured along the seat tube. This number is only a starting point, so fine-tune it based on experience. (For another method to determine your saddle height, see chapter 1.) For instance, riders with long feet and those who pedal toes down usually require a higher saddle. A helpful rule is that a saddle that's too high may cause pain in the back of the knee, while one that's too low usually produces pain in the front.

Saddle setback, or fore/aft position, is best adjusted with the bike on a stationary trainer. Sit normally, hands draped over the brake hoods, with pedals horizontal. Get someone to drop a plumb line from the front of your forward kneecap. It should touch the end of the crankarm. The result should be the center of your knee joint over the center of the pedal.

Aligning your cleats is a key aspect of proper riding position. "Poor cleat alignment is the biggest source of knee problems," notes Arnie Baker, M.D., national masters champion and a *Bicycling* magazine fitness advisory board member.

In the days of slotted cleats mated to pedals with toe clips and straps, knee injuries were less common. You rode for an hour in a new pair of cleatless shoes, then nailed the cleats to the line made on the sole by the pedal cage. Even if alignment was imperfect, old-fashioned shoes and cleats had some knee-saving play. "There were no recorded iliotibial band problems requiring surgery before step-in pedals became popular," says Dr. Pruitt. "The old cleats wore quickly, and the leather shoes didn't have a rigid heel counter, so 'float' was built in."

Now with stiff heel counters, even on pedal systems featuring rotational movement or float, proper alignment is crucial. Get your cleat position checked by a cycling coach or at a bike shop that uses the Fit Kit's Rotational Adjustment Device. Dr. Pruitt recommends pedal systems that provide at least 6 degrees of rotation (but not more than 15 degrees in

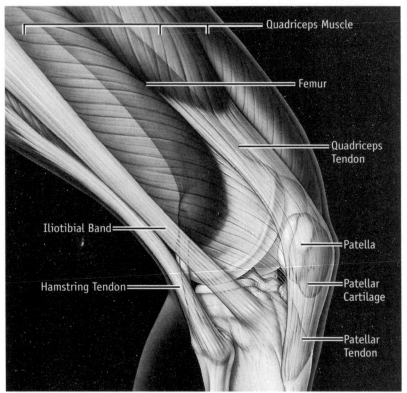

Proper care of the knee joint is essential to long-term cycling.

most cases), an end point to this movement (release point), and the ability to adjust the cleat to an individual rider's neutral position.

ON YOUR BIKE

There is a lot you can do while riding to minimize the wear and tear on your knees. Here are some tips.

Keep your knees toasty. Riding in 40°F with red, chapped knees is a recipe for trouble. Pros routinely cover their legs in training when the temperature is below 65°F. Of course, you will often see riders with bare legs on cold, windy spring days—and they never seem to get hurt. As in all things physical, there is plenty of individual variation. Dr. Baker says, "I don't cover my knees automatically whenever it drops below 65°F, and no scientific studies have shown that it's necessary, but I wouldn't discourage it."

Warm up. Ripping out of the parking lot in the big ring and putting the hammer down on the first hill is a training ride tradition that ought to be gracefully retired. Your knees need at least 15 minutes of gradual warmup. Pedal gently in smooth circles to get the blood flowing.

Spin. Look at tapes of the pros in action. You will probably be struck by the rapid and fluid pedal strokes of the best riders. Even while climbing or time trialing, activities that make weekend warriors labor at 60 to 80 revolutions per minute, pros turn closer to 100. Here's a great drill: Next time you are going up your favorite hill, use a gear at least two teeth lower than usual. If you normally climb in a 39 × 21-tooth (39 × 21T) gear, try a 24T and spin. You will probably climb just as fast, and your knees will feel better. Your leg muscles will like it, too.

Build mileage gradually. "Doing too much too fast is a common source of knee problems," Dr. Baker says. It used to be called spring knee, mild tendinitis on the top of the kneecap from riding too far on that first warm day. The standard recommendation is to increase your total mileage no more than 10 percent per week.

Beware of change. Your body likes consistency, so when you alter equipment, your knees often protest. Installing longer crankarms for a time trial, for instance, or riding a tandem with a wider bottom bracket can often precipitate knee discomfort. Whenever you make a change, go easy to give yourself time to adapt.

Don't ride a fixed-gear bike. There goes your track career. But most fixed-gear bikes lack brakes, so slowing is done by resisting the pedals. This strains the patella.

Stand tall. Don't grind up hills while seated. When your cadence falls, stand as much as possible even if you are a more-efficient climber in the saddle. The more you stand to climb, the better you will become at it.

Buy the correct inserts. Don't use rear-posted orthotics (custom shoe inserts). These are made for running and aren't helpful for cyclists. Instead, get front-posted orthotics that extend to below the ball of the foot.

Don't use a fixed-position pedal/cleat system. For most knees, float is better because it relieves stress by helping feet find their natural position on the pedals.

OFF YOUR BIKE

Protect your knees when you are off the bike, too. The following rules don't apply equally to everyone, however. Consider, for example, squats with a barbell. Some people can do full squats for years and never have trouble. Others get chondromalacia (irritation on the back of the kneecap) from squatting to tie their shoes. In applying these rules, know yourself, use common sense, and minimize the risks.

Don't squat or kneel unnecessarily. The squatting movement loads the back of the patella, while kneeling pushes it into the femoral groove, possibly damaging its smooth surface.

Take your time. Don't run up or down stairs or hills. Running downhill is particularly hard on knees. Even mountain runners, accustomed to steep 5-mile descents, practice until they can bear the brunt of the pounding with their quadriceps muscles.

Go easy on certain weight training. Don't do weight exercises such as full-range leg extensions or presses that load the patella. On extensions limit movement to the final 25 degrees before your knees straighten. Don't bend knees more than 90 degrees when doing leg presses.

Head to the doc. Do get expert help if, despite following this advice, knee pain persists.

Straight Talk about Six Cycling Problems

FOR MEN ONLY

By Gary Legwold

For most male cyclists the reproductive system is the first thing on the saddle but the last thing on our minds. And it shows. We wear helmets, shades, and gloves to protect our heads, eyes, and hands. We shave our legs, massage our muscles, and devote endless hours to maximizing our cardiorespiratory systems.

But what do we do for our poor penises and their supporting casts? Stuff them all into a pair of hot, tight, stinky shorts where they are scrunched and jiggled for hours.

Sometimes we pay supremely for this neglect. On day 11 of a coast-to-coast tour, cyclist David Mitchell bumped another bike in a paceline and crashed. In pain, he managed to ride 15 miles to a hospital. He was examined and released with four broken ribs and a banged-up pelvis.

"I could hardly walk, but I could pedal," says Mitchell, then 47. Although he couldn't stand on the bike pedals and had to lean heavily on his aero bar because of the rib pain, Mitchell averaged 140 miles each of the next 10 days to finish the 3,000-mile tour.

"I got home, having been away 21 days, and, obviously, I wanted to show my wife how much I missed her," says Mitchell, a cabinet builder from the Midwest. Trouble was, he was numb. "I could have an erection, but there was no sensation. You could have shut a car door on it, and I wouldn't have felt it."

This was in early October. After a few days of continued dormancy, Mitchell went to a urologist, who determined that the far-forward position he had ridden in had put too much pressure on the nerves of his nether region, deadening them. It would take time for the nerves to recover. Until then, the bike was off-limits.

October passed. November passed. Then, on the evening of December 22, Mitchell felt a glorious tingle, like blood returning to a foot that had fallen asleep. "I got what I wanted for Christmas," he says.

As this happy ending demonstrates, most of the unsettling situations male cyclists encounter are relatively harmless. This is some solace, but let's face facts. Even minor problems involving this sensitive area are, at best, uncomfortable, embarrassing, and alarming.

One worrisome report comes from two Danish doctors who surveyed 800 racing cyclists and found that 350 had difficulty obtaining an erection for several days after an event, and that 200 suffered from reduced "sexual sensation."

But you don't have be a megamiler to disrupt your system. Done improperly, even casual cycling (including stationary pedaling) can cause problems ranging from temporary penile numbness to infertility. Renowned urologist Irwin Goldstein, M.D., has reported cases of men becoming impotent because of injuries resulting from falls onto the bike's top tube or stem. Even more alarming is his contention that impotence may occur due to compression of penile nerves and blood vessels from the mere act of sitting on a saddle.

But hold on. Before all the color drains from your face, keep in mind that simple precautions prevent many of these problems, and most others can be resolved. Cycling and sex aren't oil and water. In fact, scientists (and many happy riders) believe that spinning your wheels can improve your sex drive.

Here are six of the most common cycling-related problems in the male reproductive system.

Penile numbness. To understand this, you must understand the prostate. The prostate is a walnut-shaped gland with muscles that contract to help squirt 2 to 4 milliliters of semen (containing 100 million to 600 million sperm) out of the penis during ejaculation. It also helps the sperm swim and keeps them safe by producing lubricating fluids that neutralize vaginal acidity. This secretion and others produced by various organs contain sugars and nutrients for the sperm. They compose most of the volume of semen (less than 10 percent is sperm).

The gland lies between the scrotum and anus, the area that has the most contact with the saddle. "The prostate is just a finger's width away when you sit on a bike seat," says H. R. Safford, M.D., a Denver urologist and a *Bicycling* magazine fitness advisory board member.

Constant proximity to the saddle can "bruise" the prostate, says Wayman Spence, M.D., in private practice in Waco, Texas, who did just that during a 500-mile ride. When this happens, the prostate swells and puts pressure on the nearby perineal, dorsal, and pudendal nerves, which feed into the penis. Numbness occurs.

If you stay off the bike, the condition usually disappears within a week with no after-effects "other than a mild loss of enthusiasm before the next ride," says Jeffrey York, M.D., of the division of urology at Ohio State University in Columbus.

The simplest way to avoid this situation is to stand on the pedals more while riding, perhaps as often as once every 15 minutes. Shift your weight on the saddle, too, and make sure it is wide enough to support you by your "sit bones." These things will minimize the pressure that inflames the prostate. (For more information, see chapter 40.)

Urinary complications. Cyclists who traumatize their prostates may also suffer from urine flow that is frequent, infrequent, bloody, or terminally dribbling, or that causes a burning sensation (thankfully not all at once, though).

These symptoms usually arise when the prostate is irritated beyond bruising to full-blown infection, or prostatitis. The infection interferes

---

BEWARE THE PROSTATE

At the first sign of urinary trouble, get a prostate-specific antigen (PSA) test, especially if you are over 40. This test to detect prostate cancer is more accurate than the check routinely given during a physical exam, which involves only the doctor feeling the prostate.

Ray Chumley, 55, a cyclist from Oregon, was told at his biannual physical that his prostate felt firm—nothing unusual for someone who rides so much, his doctor said. But because firmness is also a potential sign of cancer, Chumley took a PSA test. He had cancer.

"The cancer had nothing to do with cycling. I don't want people deluded here," says Chumley. "The point is that cyclists could get a wrong diagnosis because of similar symptoms. So get the PSA."

An estimated 244,000 men develop prostate cancer in the United States each year. About 40,000 die—the second highest number of cancer deaths in men (behind lung cancer).

Chumley's cancer was detected early, and the gland was removed. Temporary impotence and incontinence followed, but he is alive—and cycling.

with the prostate's ability to monitor the reproductive system's fluid output, and strange things begin happening. The cure is simple: antibiotics and time off the bike. Two weeks of each is usually enough.

Bloody urine also occurs in endurance events. The kidneys can bleed because they "just work too hard" reabsorbing water, filtering blood, and excreting waste, explains Dr. Spence.

And during jarring activities, such as riding rough roads or mountain biking, the walls of an empty bladder can bump against each other and bleed, says Dr. York. It's just one more reason to stay well-hydrated.

Scary as these problems appear, they are usually harmless displays—smoke bombs as opposed to hand grenades—created by the body to get your attention and warn you to stop an activity that could lead to permanent damage. But these symptoms can also be caused by ailments (such as kidney infection or bladder cancer) that are far more dangerous, even life-threatening. For this reason it's best to assume that urinary problems aren't caused by cycling. See a doctor. If the diagnosis blames your bike, be glad. The only immediate danger is that you will get bored because you can't ride.

Inadvertent discharges. Urologists occasionally hear from guys who, in roundabout and somewhat tentative language, ask if they know of any condition that might cause male cyclists to ejaculate while riding.

Is there such a condition, or do these guys love cycling more than the rest of us?

Dr. York says that the motion of the legs and hips during pedaling can sometimes create an indirect form of prostatic massage. When this happens, the gland is "milked" and emits fluid. It's not ejaculation (no sperm is delivered from the testicles), just a sticky discharge of the prostate's lubricating liquid.

The remedy, says Dr. Safford, is to reduce the fluid pressure inside the prostate with masturbation or intercourse. Tough medicine.

Testicular trauma. Most males are surprised yet grateful that the testicles don't get traumatized more often in cycling.

Each of these complex organs comprises 275 yards of delicate coiled tubes that make sperm. These seminiferous tubules lead to the epididymis, a 20-foot coiled structure behind each testicle in which sperm mature. The spermatic cord ascends from this coil to the urethra (the tube running from the bladder), through the prostate, and out the penis. The cord contains blood vessels and the vas deferens, the tube that transports sperm (and the one that's cut in a vasectomy).

Despite the fact that cycling buffets these free-hanging and sensitive organs between pumping thighs and bounces them on the bike seat, they aren't harmed. Credit some of this safe passage to bicycle shorts. Like jockstraps, they provide some protection by compacting and containing the package.

But in a crash this same tightness can work against us. Because the scrotum can't swing freely on impact, it may be more susceptible to injury. Dr. York had a patient who was involved in a crash, causing one testicle to become trapped between saddle and bone. The testicle ruptured, and part of it had to be removed. No doubt the pain was excruciating, but even here the news is relatively good. Losing one testicle in a wreck won't make you infertile. The other can often supply enough sperm to compensate.

Penile injury. Accidents can damage the reproductive system in other ways. Because the penis extends from the body, it can be hurt during a crash.

Dr. York has treated cyclists who fell on their handlebars and damaged the blood vessels in the penis, resulting in the ability to have only a partial erection. An erection happens when these vessels fill with blood and widen. It is maintained by muscles that contract and trap the blood.

In Dr. York's patients, blood entered the vessels but leaked through the damaged artery wall into adjacent veins and back out of the penis. This caused partial limpness. The remedy is to surgically block the damaged artery, allowing the remaining ones to produce and maintain an erection.

Impotency and infertility. This is the big one, the grandaddy of all fears: Can cycling sap your sexual prowess?

Yes, especially if you consider the broadest definition of impotency, which is the "inability to maintain an erection that's mutually satisfactory for both partners," says Dr. York. In a heterosexual relationship this wide-ranging term can be applied any time the man either doesn't get it up or keep it up long enough for intercourse. So technically, any of the problems we have discussed could lead to impotency.

This condition affects most men sometime in their lives, says Dr. York, but cycling is not a common cause. Often impotency is psychological in origin (from stress, anxiety, guilt, or depression) or caused by such physical complications as diabetes, alcoholism, smoking, or certain medications. Impotency is correctible through various means, including the use of drugs, devices, or surgery.

Infertility is different. It refers to the inability to conceive. (Fifteen percent of couples of childbearing age are infertile.) Among the many things that can contribute to male infertility are infections, injuries, a general failure to produce enough sperm, and, yes, cycling.

Evidence is sketchy, but scientists know that under certain conditions cycling, like other endurance sports, can reduce testosterone levels. This is important because testosterone, a hormone produced in cells between the seminiferous tubules, is responsible for sperm development and male characteristics, such as the growth of sex organs, distribution of body hair (including baldness), deepening of the voice, and muscle growth.

In one study Ruddy Dressendorfer, Ph.D., director of the exercise science laboratory at New Mexico Highlands University in Las Vegas, New Mexico, measured testosterone in marathoners who doubled their regular mileage during 15 days of racing. The levels fell by 31 percent. This is consistent with other research involving cyclists, rowers, runners, and swimmers that showed a 20 to 30 percent drop in testosterone after intense and prolonged (more than 2 hours) exercise.

Scientists are also beginning to suspect that, aside from sudden training increases, long-term participation in sports such as cycling may also lower testosterone. In a published study Mary Jane De Souza, Ph.D., who works at the University of Connecticut Health Center in Farmington, checked sperm quality and testosterone in established runners (60-plus miles per week), weight trainers (2-plus hours, four-plus days per week), and a control group of average men. In both exercise groups testosterone levels were about 25 percent lower than in the controls. In the runners sperm count, motility, and its ability to penetrate the cervical mucus were lower, and there were more immature sperm cells.

Why such differences? "We don't know," says Dr. De Souza. The jarring that occurs during exercise may negatively affect testicle cells. Others theorize that anxiety and stress may influence the part of the brain that regulates the production of testosterone. One extra problem for cyclists may be that their testicles are hampered inside hot shorts. Testicles need a cool environment to thrive. This is why males have scrotums—to keep testicles cooler than body temperature.

Despite the undeniable dive in this important hormone, it's important to remember that no clear-cut evidence links moderate cycling to infertility. Also keep in mind that the decreases caused by increased riding seem to be temporary. Testosterone levels return to normal with a week of rest or reduced training. Anyway, the drop-off may not matter. Even with lower testosterone levels, most cyclists are still fertile. Only men whose sperm counts are normally low face possible infertility from a further decrease.

"It's important not to send an alarming message," says Dr. Dressendorfer. "You can do very heavy training and still be fertile."

REALITY CHECK

Now take a deep breath and relax. After all the dire warnings, it's time for perspective.

Although no definite numbers are available, researchers and doctors estimate that only a tiny percentage of male cyclists ride long enough or hard enough to paralyze their penises, become impotent, or suffer any of the other horrors that have been discussed.

And even the few studies issuing warnings to the hammerheads seem to be inconclusive and outweighed by anecdotal evidence indicating the opposite effect. The Danish study, for instance, was quickly disputed by pro cycling's medical commissions and racers.

The best news is that moderate cycling can improve your sex drive. Loren Cordain, Ph.D., from the department of exercise and sports science at Colorado State University in Fort Collins, says, "There is no doubt that when a sedentary person takes up moderate exercise, libido is enhanced."

Compared with sedentary sorts, exercisers usually have better circulation, sleep, diets, and flexibility, and can elevate their endorphins (one of the hormones that make us feel pleasure) to higher levels. These are pluses for sexual pleasure. Exercisers also tend to have less fat. Dr. York says that fat contributes to the production of estrogen (a feminizing hormone). A high level can depress sex drives in men by countering the masculinizing effects of testosterone.

Perhaps the biggest benefit of exercise on libido is to the mind. In his book, The Exercise Habit, James Gavin, Ph.D., cites surveys that found that people are more aroused after exercise, wanted (and got) more sex the more they exercised, and maintained sexual activity longer into old age. A big reason is that "exercise gets you to live in your body, not just on top of it with your mind," says Dr. Gavin, a sports psychologist at Concordia University in Montreal. "Hundreds of studies show that exercise improves self-esteem," which improves sex. In plainer words, he says, "If you feel like crap, you don't feel sexy."

So ride with confidence. Cycling helps not only your head and overall health but also your sex life. Just remember to respect your reproductive system. Take care of it, and when the time comes, it will take care of you.

FOR WOMEN ONLY

**By *Bicycling* Magazine's
Fitness Advisory Board**

It's not just men who wonder about possible physical side effects from cycling. Women have their own unique questions, too. And while many of these questions don't pertain to the reproductive system, they're just as important. In this chapter medical experts provide answers to the most-frequent questions women have about cycling.

Q. I'm a serious cyclist, and I'm also pregnant. Will it be harmful to me or to the baby if I continue to ride hard?

A. Cycling is an excellent aerobic activity for pregnant women. Research indicates that there's no harm to mother or child when you elevate your heart rate to your anaerobic threshold. Although I don't recommend interval training, it isn't a problem to jam the occasional hill. In general, keep your heart rate between 65 and 75 percent of your maximum.

Pregnant women do not dissipate excess body heat as readily as nonpregnant women. So take the extra precautions of riding in the cooler hours of the day, drinking every 15 minutes, and going more slowly when it's hot. No special foods are necessary. Just be sure to eat regularly and stay hydrated.

—Camilla Buchanan, M.D.

Q. I purchased a bike trailer so that I can take my one-year-old son on rides. At this point he can only tolerate an hour, which allows us to do 12 to 15 miles five times a week

**in hilly terrain. How can I get the most effi-
cient workout within these time and mileage
constraints?**

A. Pulling a trailer is a good workout. In hilly terrain every pedal
stroke can be like a leg press. The first priority is to gear your bike low
enough with a large rear cog and triple crankset. Your knees will thank
you.

As for training methods, I don't recommend intervals or high-intensity regimens with a trailer. Such an approach will trash you, and
it's harder to control the trailer at high speeds, which may endanger
your child. Instead, think of a trailer ride as power training. It will develop muscle and may even contribute to better time trials, but it won't
do much for your acceleration or leg speed. For that you need to
schedule time for riding alone and doing intervals or sprints. Perhaps
you can do them on a stationary trainer while you keep an eye on
Junior.

When your son is in the trailer, make sure that he's having fun.
Transform it into a veritable Romper Room by including a water bottle,
snacks, toys, books, or plush animals. When my daughter was little, the
longest ride we used to take was about 2½ hours, including a stop at a
park. She loved going in the trailer because we made it fun.

In general, think of the trailer as a family experience that provides
fitness as a bonus, not the reverse.

—Geoff Drake

**Q. I seem to sweat very little compared with
my cycling companions. In fact, on hot days I
overheat and need to slow down. My doctor gave
me a clean bill of health and said that my
problem is due to individual differences.
Should I accept this situation and continue
riding in my club's 13-mile-per-hour category,
or is there something I can do to move up to 16
miles per hour?**

A. Many women don't sweat as much as men. Instead, they rely on
their cardiovascular system to move body heat to the skin surface for
dissipation. This works fine, but it can strain the system when it's very
warm. This is what you are feeling when you say that you have to slow
down.

You should enhance your cardiovascular efficiency with a training program. Three times a week for 30 minutes or more, ride at about 75 percent of your maximum heart rate. These workouts will eventually increase your blood volume and heat tolerance, enabling you to join the faster riders.

—Christine Wells, Ph.D.

Q. Is it okay to ride during my period?

A. Women were once urged to avoid exercising (and even to avoid polite company) during "certain times of the month." A woman was taught to be more delicate and less stable during her period. "We may have been socialized to believe that we are too fragile to exercise vigorously, especially during our periods," says Diane Wakat, Ph.D., professor of health education at the University of Virginia in Charlottesville.

But science does not support this belief. For example, the production of lactic acid (a substance in the muscles that inhibits performance) is no greater during menstruation, and we know that women—including cyclists—have set records and won Olympic medals during all phases of their menstrual cycles.

Still, many women feel tired or less enthusiastic about their workouts at specific times each month. Such fatigue or malaise varies widely from woman to woman, and science can't readily account for it. For those who experience it, doctors usually recommend charting cycles for several months and noting those times when you are least inspired to exercise. Then, simply plan to train lightly or rest on those days.

If menstrual cramping interferes with cycling, many women find that the nonprescription drug ibuprofen helps so well that they can exercise without difficulty shortly after taking the recommended dosage.

While menstruation should have little effect on your cycling, there is debate as to what cycling can do to menstruation. Some doctors have claimed that strenuous training will disrupt a woman's cycle, interfering with her fertility and possibly her health. In certain cases women athletes have stopped having their periods, a condition known as amenorrhea. It won't permanently affect the ability to become pregnant, but amenorrhea may influence how the body stores calcium. No period means little or no estrogen production, and estrogen is essential for calcium storage. Consequently, amenorrheic women are thought to be at greater risk of developing osteoporosis.

But the connection between exercise and amenorrhea is still being researched. "Do athletes become amenorrheic because they are athletes or because of other factors?" asks Anne Loucks, Ph.D., assistant research endocrinologist at the University of California in San Diego. "Women athletes tend to be thin. They tend to shun certain foods. They may be anxious about competition. The so-called athletic lifestyle may contribute more to the development of amenorrhea than the actual exercise."

Likewise, the ramifications of the condition itself are also suspect. "The prevailing explanation of amenorrhea has defined it as a disease," says one doctor, "whereas our research indicates it is an adaptation and a perfectly healthy one. If a woman athlete is amenorrheic now but wants to become pregnant later, she can. Her reproductive system has not changed permanently."

It's interesting to note that in most studies, the athletes who developed menstrual irregularities were serious runners. Few cyclists had problems. But if your period does change, either after you begin riding regularly or after you increase your mileage, see a doctor—preferably a gynecologist who is familiar with athletic amenorrhea.

—Editors of *Bicycling* magazine

Q. I'm sometimes incapacitated by menstrual-like cramps during cycling and other aerobic sports even when I'm between periods. The cramps generally last for 10 minutes, after which I can resume exercising without a recurrence. What is causing this problem?

A. This cramping is uncommon but not unheard of. I have two patients with a similar history. I'll assume that your family doctor and gynecologist have examined you and found nothing abnormal.

All cramping, including menstrual, results from a contracting muscle. During menstruation, a hormone is produced that causes the uterine muscles to contract. It's possible that exercise prompts your body to produce this hormone at other times in your cycle. Try taking 400 to 800 milligrams of ibuprofen before exercising. This should keep the muscles from contracting involuntarily.

—Camilla Buchanan, M.D.

Q. I have been diagnosed with chondromalacia and malalignment syndrome of the patella. An orthopedist told me that women are often born

with malaligned kneecaps. Is there anything I can do while cycling to correct this?

A. It seems true that more women than men are "knock-kneed," the common term for valgus knee alignment. Many times this condition accompanies the wide, shallow pelvis of the female, and yes, this type of knee alignment produces a greater incidence of chondromalacia (damage to the underside of the kneecap) as well as osteoarthritis.

The keys to minimizing the problem in cycling are: (1) proper bike fit, (2) a saddle position set as high as possible before the hips begin to rock, (3) clipless pedals that allow the feet a few degrees of float (unrestricted rotation) before release, and (4) gears low enough to allow an 85-plus pedaling cadence as much as possible.

If your malalignment is severe, surgery can help correct it and possibly prevent future swelling and pain. The good news is that cycling is a recommended activity for your condition—if you follow the aforementioned rules. It is my experience that 90 percent of those who suffer from chondromalacia can ride comfortably at some level.

—Andrew Pruitt, Ed.D.

Q. My vagina gets sore when riding long distances. The skin breaks and sometimes bleeds. The padding in cycling shorts seems to wick moisture away and make things worse. I've tried using Vaseline and Noxema, but the improvement is minimal. What do other women do?

A. Yours is a universal problem. We can only minimize, not totally eliminate, abrasions to the vulva (lips around the vagina). This problem is worse, however, if your saddle is too high. Have your position checked at a bike shop. Even if the height is within the recommended range, try lowering it 5 millimeters.

Also check the saddle's tilt by laying a yardstick on it from front to back. If it's not perfectly level or pointed down slightly, the saddle can put excessive pressure on your crotch.

Sit so the outside of the vulva contacts the saddle. The skin of this hair-covered area is more durable than the inner lips. Change positions frequently on every ride. A more upright position, with hands on the top of the handlebar, tends to shift weight off the most sensitive areas.

In addition, make sure you wear high-quality shorts. Remove them as soon as possible after riding, then shower. If painful abrasions occur despite these measures, get a prescription for sulfadiazine cream from your gynecologist. It works for me.

—Camilla Buchanan, M.D.

Q. It seems that the more I ride, the more bladder infections I get. Why does cycling cause this?

A. Any activity that traumatizes the female urethra increases the risk of bacteria entering the bladder and infecting the urinary tract. Prolonged contact with a bicycle saddle could provoke an infection in a woman who is susceptible.

Some simple measures, however, can reduce the concentration of bacteria in the bladder and help prevent infections. Drink plenty of fluid while riding. Empty your bladder every 2 hours while cycling and as soon as possible afterward. If infections continue, ask your doctor to prescribe a prophylactic antibiotic.

—Camilla Buchanan, M.D.

Q. On long, hot rides I get the equivalent of male jock itch. If I stay off my bike for a week, it clears up with the help of cortisone pills. But nothing prevents recurrences. What can I do?

A. Your problem is probably prickly heat, a type of rash. Try loose-fitting shorts that allow better air circulation in the crotch. At the first sign of a rash, try an over-the-counter hydrocortisone cream. Cool compresses immediately after riding might help, too, as would a postride swim. You could also try changing shorts in the middle of a ride.

—Christine Wells, Ph.D.

Q. I'm 40 and experiencing fluid buildup in my legs after rides, especially long and hard ones. I have consulted a medical doctor, vascular surgeon, chiropractor, massage therapist, and physical therapist. No one has a clue. Do you?

A. Minor fluid buildup (edema) is common in women. There is a variety of conditions (some serious) that can lead to this problem.

These range from potassium depletion to heart or kidney failure. If your edema is as great as it sounds, you should certainly be evaluated by an internal medicine specialist. Assuming that you are found negative for any known condition, there are two treatments: support stockings or diuretics. The former are custom-fitted and tighter in the feet than in the legs, so fluid is squeezed upward to eventually be eliminated by the kidneys. Diuretics have few side effects for the casual cyclist, but do require monitoring by a physician.

—David Smith, M.D.

Q. I'm 30, approximately 50 pounds overweight, and haven't been on a bike since I was a child. I would like to start cycling for fitness and pleasure, but I have no idea where to begin. Help!

A. Start by adopting a high-carbohydrate, low-fat diet. Omit fried foods and baked goods, add lots of fresh fruit and vegetables, and eat red meat sparingly if at all.

Start taking easy rides in a low gear. Make cycling 10 miles in 1 hour your goal, and then gradually increase your speed and distance (about 2 miles at a time) as you become fit. Two common mistakes made by beginners are trying to keep pace with more accomplished riders and pedaling in a gear that's too high. To avoid these pitfalls, do your own thing at your own speed. Ride three or four times a week. Stick with this program until your weight decreases and your fitness and skill increase. Then begin riding with others to expand your knowledge and ability.

—Christine Wells, Ph.D.

Q. I rode my first century last year. While training for it, my legs became large and I wasn't able to reduce my waist measurement. Can't cycling help my legs stay trim?

A. Don't be afraid of developing a little muscle. You may find that your unused leg muscles will develop before you begin to lose fat. The best way to reduce your waist and not develop large legs is to do endurance riding all year. This means spinning with low pedal resistance and high revolutions (at least 90 revolutions per minute). Stay at about 70 percent of your maximum heart rate. In this way you will burn plenty of calories but without the high intensity that develops greater muscle size.

If weight loss is your goal, remember that cutting fat from your diet is important. But don't count calories when you are doing endurance cycling, or you will run low on energy and enthusiasm.

—Christine Wells, Ph.D.

Q. What can a woman do about the discomfort of sitting on a bicycle seat?

A. Most bike frames are designed for male proportions (leg, arm, trunk). But women are not merely small men. Our proportions are different. So simply buying a small frame usually doesn't work. Frequently, the top tube is too long. This makes you reach for the handlebar, forcing weight onto your pubic bone. No saddle will feel comfortable with that happening.

The best solution is to ride a bicycle designed for women. Otherwise, search for a conventional model that fits. Visit a bike shop that uses the Fit Kit or another sizing system to get expert advice on the frame proportions right for your body.

The second issue is body posture—how you sit on the saddle. Make sure that your arms bear a good portion of your weight. If you were to weigh a bike ridden by a correctly positioned cyclist, you would find that about 40 percent of her total weight is on the front wheel while 60 percent is on the rear. Many cyclists suffer saddle problems because their rear percentage is too high. Distribute more weight to the front by putting your handlebar at least 1 inch lower than the seat.

Also, it's best to use a woman's saddle. You will see several brands and designs at a well-stocked bike shop. They will be anatomically shaped to support and cushion a woman's wider pelvic bones. Some contain gel or liquid for improved cushioning. When the saddle is installed, its top should be level or angled slightly down toward the front, never up.

—Christine Wells, Ph.D.

Q. I have seen ads touting bikes that are built especially for a female's proportions. Is this just hype or something I should seriously consider?

A. When I started riding at age 15, there wasn't much to bike sizing. You bought any frame you could straddle; you rode bent way over like the guys, and if it hurt, well, it hurt. Eventually, I switched to a shorter stem to ease the ache in my back, but that was the only concession I made. When other female riders complained of seat or neck or shoulder pain, I thought, "What wimps!" and told them, "You'll get used to it."

Some did. Some didn't. I was lucky. I'm tall, with long arms and slim hips, so my bike fits better than most women's. But all women aren't built alike—and we're not built like men. Most women have a proportionately shorter torso and longer legs, a wider pelvis, and less upper-body strength than men. So even if a bike fits your leg length, its top tube, stem, and cranks could be too long, and its saddle could be too narrow.

So what happens if your bike doesn't fit? Probably nothing bad if you cruise only a few miles around the neighborhood. But if you crank up the mileage, you can suffer back, neck, hip, or butt pain, in varying degrees of severity. And your pedaling efficiency can suffer, too.

As those ads say, some manufacturers are addressing this issue, and these are some of their considerations.

Frame. Based on their shorter torsos, women tend to need a shorter top tube. But if the rider is small enough—say, under 5-foot-4—the top tube can be so short that her forward shoe will overlap the front wheel when the crankarms are horizontal. This can cause contact (and possibly a crash) if the rider turns her wheel too sharply. Some manufacturers resolve this problem by using a smaller front wheel. Georgena Terry, founder of Terry Precision Cycling for Women, uses a 24-inch front and a standard 700C rear on her 16-, 17.5-, and 19-inch road bikes. This trick also allows the smaller bikes to retain a relatively normal head angle of 71 to 72 degrees for predictable steering. It's also important to have the correct seat tube angle to ensure that the saddle (and subsequently your legs) is in the correct fore/aft position in relation to the pedals. (Moving the saddle back and forth enables you to fine-tune this.) Generally, people with longer thighs want 72- or 73-degree seat angles, while short-thigh folks look for angles a bit steeper to move them farther over the pedals.

Stem. The oldest trick in the book is to compensate for a too-long top tube by installing a shorter stem. This brings the bar closer to the seat. Some manufacturers, such as Nitto, make stems that come with very short extensions. Most shops can obtain one to fit you. (They come as small as 4 centimeters, measured from the stem bolt to handlebar center.)

Handlebar. Women's shoulders tend to be narrower than men's, and a bar that's too wide can cause upper back, shoulder, or neck pain. Terry offers 36- and 38-centimeter-wide handlebars rather than the more standard 40-centimeter, and the Terry T-bar has a recessed area in the hooks that shortens the reach to the brake levers.

Crankarms. For the road 160- to 165-millimeter cranks rather than the standard 170-millimeter (indicated on the back of the crankarm) are usually a better fit for those with an inseam of less than 29½ inches (measured from crotch to floor in bare feet). If you have a mountain bike that you ride off-road, its crankarms should be 5 millimeters longer than the correct size for your road bike, for better leverage on climbs.

Saddle. Check out the new models that are actually cut out where one's private parts would touch. These are made by Terry and Selle San Marco.

Brake levers. Because they have smaller hands and shorter fingers, many women need short-reach brake levers, such as those from Dia-Compe and Shimano.

So, with all of these component options to alter an off-the-rack model, do you really need a woman's bike? Some folks like me—5-foot-9 with long arms—can manage on men's frames that have top tubes slightly shorter than average, or by installing a shorter stem. Racers and triathletes striving for the most streamlined position likely will prefer a bike that stretches them out more. You can adjust any bike to fit better in length, as long as its height is right. (When you stand over the top tube, you should have at least 2 inch of crotch clearance.)

Tradeoffs exist, however, when making equipment and position changes. A saddle shoved too far forward can cause inefficient pedaling and knee problems. A too-short stem can result in squirrelly bike handling—as I learned when I switched to a bike with a shorter top tube and longer stem, then discovered that I wasn't the rotten bike handler I thought I was. And for some unlucky people, all the adjustments in the world won't make them much more comfortable.

The biggest advantages to riding a bike designed for women come to those under 5-foot-4. The tubes on some of these frames are 10 percent smaller in diameter than those used for a midsize frame, which takes some harshness out of the ride. Explains Stewart Shaffer of Serotta Cycles, a maker of women's bikes, "If you take the big tubes that we use for a 190-pound rider and stick them under a 110-pound person, it's going to beat them up more."

The Cannondale R600C compact road bike has a 1.6-inch-diameter seat tube, about 0.6-inch less than that of its larger bikes. This model comes in 43- to 49-centimeter frames, with 650C wheels in the smaller sizes, plus narrower handlebars and 165-millimeter cranks. The 43-centimeter version has a 75-degree seat-tube angle and 72-degree head-tube angle. "It handles like a full-size bike would for a large person," says Chris Petron of Cannondale. "It's not marketed specifically to women but is popular among women and does well in Japan."

Terry is unique in offering frames to fit women as tall as 5-foot-11, not just those under 5-foot-4. Says the owner, "Women's muscles are not only generally smaller but are distributed differently, resulting in more force on joints. A slightly more upright riding position eases those forces."

Does every woman need a woman's bike? Maybe not, but we all could use a bike that fits, particularly in the top tube—and a woman's bike isn't a bad place to start looking.

—Sara J. Henry

EIGHT

Special
Bikes

Sit Back and Take a Spin

THE RAD WORLD OF RECUMBENTS

By Jim Langley

A t age 61, Bill Cook rediscovered cycling. A writer for *U.S. News and World Report* in Washington, D.C., he's not just pedaling, though. Says Cook, "I took a welding course, bought a torch, air compressor, drill press, CAD program and book on how to build bikes, spent a day with a master framebuilder in Japan watching him make frames, and I built a framebuilding jig." With this set up, Cook has constructed eight bikes, including one for a friend. And he is still designing, tinkering, and experimenting—trying to build a "better bicycle."

Miles away in Dayton, Ohio, the powers that be at Huffy Bicycle Company, the largest manufacturer of two-wheelers in America, share Cook's enthusiasm. In a significant departure from their bread and butter (knocking out zillions of entry-level bikes), they recently purchased and have begun manufacturing Re-Bikes, models that share many of the design characteristics of Cook's creations. Bill Smith, vice president of marketing, explains, "It's a unique product niche that has future potential because it appeals to a very diverse group of people."

Way west, Jim Wronski, a Los Angeles–based bike dealer, has switched over most of the inventory in his store to this new breed of bike. He's not the only one. Chris Kegel, owner of five bike shops in Milwaukee, is on the bandwagon big time, even working with a manufacturer called Linear to produce a new model.

What has all these folks in a tizzy? Recumbents. Those weird-science sleds that are a little bit La-Z-Boy, little bit NASA. Think of them as a chaise lounge with wheels. The name *recumbent* comes from the reclining, feet-first riding position, and owners are fond of calling themselves bent. That's not surprising for a group that's as outspoken as their

Recumbents add a new dimension to cycling.

bikes are bizarre. Like religious zealots or insurance salesmen, these folks are nothing if not fervent. They are ingenious inventors, folks who just want to be different, speed junkie–kamikaze pilots, and people who cannot ride regular bikes due to medical problems.

Take Jerry Lobdill. In his mid-fifties he was ready to quit riding because of numbness in his palms and crotch, and an aching neck. Then he tried a recumbent. He crows, "The very first trip I doubled the distance I'd ever been able to achieve on my wedgie [traditional bike], and wonder of wonders, I had no numbness. Since then, I've logged another 4,000 miles."

Bruce Buttimore is a software engineer and glider pilot. He raves, "Upright bikes fail on most of the key design requirements. They are uncomfortable, their design causes high wind drag, there's poor forward visibility, and safety is marginal. Your body is high off the ground and panic stops can land you on your head."

Adds a convert named Bruce Bruemmer, "I have had 10-year-old boys running out of their houses yelling 'cool bike' at me. I've had a van follow me taking photographs, tough guys on Harleys cheering me on, and people just bursting out in laughter. Half of me wishes that more people would discover the joys of recumbency, the other half hopes to keep it my little secret."

These folks may sound eccentric, but they are part of a growing

(continued on page 202)

A CONVERT'S TALE

During my first 25 years in cycling, I can remember sitting on a recumbent just once. It was inside a bike shop, so I couldn't have ridden it if I wanted to. I didn't want to. To me, a die-hard road bike aficionado, recumbents were interesting but vaguely distasteful, like the freak show on the fringe of a carnival's midway.

Then, in a classic case of irony, a medical condition made a conventional saddle very unappealing to me. I loved cycling too much to stop, so the only way I could keep going was—gulp!—on a recumbent.

Not knowing which of the many designs might be best, I tried three. It turns out that each would be a charter member if there were a recumbent hall of fame: the Ryan Vanguard, the P-38 Lightning, and the Gold Rush by Easy Racers. Each bike's design dates from the 1980s, the dawn of the modern recumbent universe. Although they are very different from each other, each is a proven and popular design. By riding all three, this old roadie got a great overview of what recumbent cycling is all about.

Comfort. This is supposed to be the number one reason to ride a recumbent: a comfortable, relaxed, head-up riding position. Well, at least your head is up. Don't let anyone tell you that switching to a recumbent will immediately remedy the aches and pains of cycling. Recumbents have their own collection, concentrated on the quads, glutes, and hip flexors. I hurt so much during some rides that I had to stop and walk. I stayed so sore that I wasn't able to ride two days in a row.

To be fair, 'bent people freely admit that it takes time to adapt to the new position. Dick Ryan and Lightning's Tim Brummer say to give it at least a month. Easy Racers' Gardner Martin says that it could be more like six months. All I know is that improvement is slow. Switching among the three bikes probably didn't help because their riding positions are distinct. Later, as I began riding just the Gold Rush, comfort increased more quickly.

Performance. After my first recumbent ride, I was concerned. I like to cycle athletically—jamming over short hills, sprinting to beat a stoplight, getting low to punch through a headwind, feeling strong to the end of 4-hour rides. On the Ryan I immediately discovered that I couldn't ride at my usual pace. Granted, the Ryan is a touring 'bent with no claim of speed. It's a fine design that *Bicycling* magazine has termed "possibly the safest and most comfortable bike in the world." But even though cruising is enjoyable, I wished there was something more.

During subsequent rides, things got better. For instance, on my first outing on the Gold Rush with its windscreen, I was able to average the same speed as on a regular bike despite some long climbs. I actually passed several first-half landmarks faster than usual, then gave back time during the hillier second half. But not much. Those who say that recumbents can't climb are only partially right. Some can't, but my experience says that others can be almost as fast as an upright. (On descents 'bents are clear winners. The Gold Rush hit 50 miles per hour on the same downhill that I top out at 47.5 miles per hour on my full-aero time trial machine, a Litespeed Blade.)

Fun. Okay, I'll admit it—recumbents are a gas. On descents the long-wheelbase Ryan, with its under-seat steering, is the closest thing you can get to street luge. Its 20-inch front wheel is so far out there that you imagine you are in a rail dragster. You start looking for a seat belt to buckle. But in most terrain this bike's riding position is designed for relaxed comfort, not speed. You sit with your arms at your sides (catching max air), and there is a large, open angle between your torso and thighs. It can't be beat, though, for riders seeking lounge-chair comfort and picture-window visibility.

The Lightning is the other extreme. Your body is closed up as though you were in a tight, aero position on your regular road bike, only rotated backward. The handlebar is barely a foot from your face. Your feet are up in your field of vision and ahead of the front wheel. The short wheelbase, plus this bike's lightness and high center of gravity, give it the handling worthy of its name. It seems built for one thing: speed. If you believe that Fast + Responsive = Fun, the Lightning fills your formula.

My favorite is the Gold Rush. For a beginning recumbent rider, it combines the best of both worlds: long-wheelbase stability with plenty of velocity. The fairing is key. Everything is behind it except your head, so you are able to see over it, not through it. (It's an effective shield against bugs, rain, and cold air, too.) The Gold Rush's riding position isn't extremely open or closed, so I had less trouble adapting my road bike muscles. It has an all-around pleasant demeanor—no handling surprises, with confident stability at speed.

For more information on these bikes, you can contact: Easy Racers, Inc., (408) 722-9797 or http://www.info@easyracers.com; Lightning Cycle Dynamics, Inc., (805) 736-0700; or Ryan Recumbent Cycles, Inc., (617) 979-0072.

—Ed Pavelka

group. Though sales of recumbents make up a tiny piece of the bike-market pie (like tandems, about 3 percent each year), there are signs suggesting far greater interest and potential for growth. For instance, a message posted on the International Human Powered Vehicle (IHPV) Internet newsgroup (http://www.ihpva.org) resulted in e-mail from hundreds of enthusiastic recumbent fans. Also, consider that along with Huffy's entry into the market there are upward of 30 small manufacturers building recumbents. Consider, too, that because recumbents are so comfortable, they are likely to appeal to millions of baby boomers who have just begun turning 50. Indeed, the growth of the recumbent market appears inevitable.

Already, strong recumbent groups have formed. One is WHIRL, which stands for Washington's (D.C.) Happily Independent Recumbent Lovers, whom Bill Cook rides with. He says, "It's not a club—it has no officers, no meetings, no bylaws—it's a start time. We ride once a week." One of the founders, Alan Pollock, describes his recumbent experience, "When you start riding a bike as a child, you do it for the fun and adventure, riding through new neighborhoods, to the store or school. It transported you into another dimension. You were riding the range as a cowboy, piloting an airplane or spacecraft, or driving a race car. Somewhere along the adult path, we lost our way, became much too serious, and started counting miles. Recumbents, for me, recapture what in the heck we started riding bicycles for in the first place."

Sentiments like this are behind clubs such as the Wisconsin/Illinois HPV riders, the Los Angeles Recumbent Riders, and the Kings of Comfort, a group in Hawaii. Of course, there's also the International Human Powered Vehicle Association (IHPVA), which includes members with all manner of remarkable recumbents including those that fly and float. The IHPVA was created because the Union Cycliste Internationale, the governing body of international racing, banned recumbents after a 'bent rider began winning professional road races and shattering records in the early 1930s. The ban effectively stagnated bicycle design. So, to re-encourage creativity, the IHPVA has put on a speed championship each summer since 1975, spurring pedal-power advocates to form HPV clubs and hold championships in countries around the world. Some of the records are amazing: top speeds of 70-plus miles per hour and distances of 49 miles in an hour, for instance.

It's another testimonial to the worthiness of recumbents. Extraordinarily comfortable for touring and commuting, too fast to be allowed to race with regular bikes, and just plain fun, their time has come.

For more information contact IHPVA, Box 727, Elgin, IL 60121, plus two publications: Recumbent Cyclist News, (206) 630-7200; and Bike Culture Quarterly, (213) 468-1080 or http.//www.bikeculture.com.

LAID-BACK LANGUAGE

It wouldn't be a new style of riding if it didn't have its own terminology. For those wedgies looking to become benders, here's how to talk the talk.

Ape hangers: The high-rise, stingray-style handlebars, or "tillers," found on some recumbents.

ASS: Above-seat steering, in contrast to under-seat steering (USS). This describes the location of the handlebar.

Bender: A recumbent rider.

'Bent: Short for recumbent.

Cheater: What wedgie riders frequently yell at benders when they're unable to keep up.

Fairing: A windshield, often transparent, that smooths the airflow around a recumbent. It can be as large as a podlike full enclosure.

Getting bent: Buying your first recumbent.

Low life: Recumbent rider.

LWB: Long-wheelbase recumbent.

Poseur pass: Speeding up to a wedgie rider on the flats and downshifting, to look like you're coasting by effortlessly.

Streamliner: Any recumbent with a full fairing.

SWB: Short-wheelbase recumbent.

USS: Under-seat steering.

Wedgie: An upright bike or its rider; refers to a pain in the rear—reminiscent of underwear wedgies—caused by narrow bike seats.

Wuffos: The people who ask benders, "Wuffo you ride that funny-lookin' bike?"

—Wade Nelson

DOUBLE YOUR FUN

By Geoff Drake

If you have never experienced the joys of riding a tandem, you may well have a few questions about these long bikes built for two. (On the other hand, if you have been on a tandem, you probably have just one question: "When can I ride it again?") First, let's answer some important questions, then look into the basics of good tandem-riding technique.

How difficult are tandems to ride? Probably not as hard as you think. The basic techniques are similar enough to riding a single bike that an experienced cyclist should have few problems acting as "captain" (the rider in front who steers). Tandem vets will tell you time and again that the key is communication. The captain should announce everything from an intention to stand to an upcoming bump. Your rear-seat "stoker," who usually can't see the road ahead and may not be a very good mind reader, will appreciate it.

Be aware. Some otherwise harmonious couples find it impossible to coexist on a tandem. The captain may be insensitive, or the stoker unwilling to surrender control. Whatever the case, it's a good reason to go for a test ride before you lay down a couple of grand for a bike that puts you in such close company. Conversely, many riders who find it impossible to ride single bikes together (usually because of a big disparity in strength or skill) have discovered that tandems are the great equalizer. They can enjoy riding together and probably go farther and faster than the weaker partner could go alone.

How much do we need to spend? Tandems are a bit like computers—you get more for less every year. Prices for complete bikes now start around

$550 to $600. Usually these are hybrid-style models, combining elements of road and mountain bikes. They may have upright handlebars, wide tires, and weigh about 50 pounds. They may also lack such amenities as "dummy" (nonfunctioning) brake levers for the stoker's hands, toe clips, or triple chainrings. They usually have relatively unsophisticated frame construction with straight-gauge tubing and perhaps no bracing. Despite these demerits, such tandems work fine for casual riding around the neighborhood, on bike paths, or at the beach.

Expect to pay $1,500 to $2,000 for a model that is suited to longer rides. Bikes in this range generally include lightweight double-butted tubing and a more sophisticated drivetrain. At prices greater than $2,000, you will see incremental improvements in components, such as clipless pedals and lightweight saddles. Also, such bikes generally have thinner, lighter tubing, leading to an overall weight of close to 40 pounds.

There is almost no price ceiling. For instance, during one model year you could blow your inheritance on the $8,300 Ibis Titanium Touche. But hey, it weighed the same as some single bikes.

What's the best frame configuration? If you go shopping for a tandem, you will notice that frame design is like an exercise in spatial geometry. Through the years manufacturers have tried running tubes up, down, and across every conceivable span. The most widely accepted design is the "direct lateral," in which a tube goes diagonally from the head tube to the rear bottom bracket (or just above it). This provides a good combination of lateral rigidity (for out-of-saddle jamming) and vertical compliance (for stoker comfort). The "uptube" design, in which a tube runs from the front bottom bracket to the intersection of tubes beneath the rear seat, also offers good rigidity for its weight, though it lacks some of the lateral stiffness of the direct lateral.

Two other designs less widely used are the "double diamond," in which the bracing tube goes from the intersection under the front seat to the rear bottom bracket, and the "open" frame, which lacks any internal bracing besides the seat tubes. Both offer a forgiving ride but will be more flexible during out-of-saddle pedaling. Keep in mind, however, that flexible frames may not seem so bad after you and your tandem partner get in sync. Also, lighter riders won't need the rigidity that heavier, frame-stressing riders will.

Should we choose 26-inch or 700C wheels? Increasingly, tandem makers specify smaller 26-inch wheels (rather than 700C, the size found on road bikes) for on- or off-road use. These are stronger, allowing the use of just 36 spokes (rather than 40 or 48, as are common for 700C-wheel tandems). When used with high-pressure road tires, these wheels roll fairly fast on tarmac. The wider 26-inch tires also absorb more road shock and are less prone to pinch flats. (Also called snakebite flats, these occur when an impact pinches the tube between the tire and rim.)

All these benefits aside, if your sole goal is to go fast on pavement, choose 700C wheels with narrow, high-pressure tires. This setup still offers the lowest rolling resistance overall.

What's the correct frame size for me and my partner? Most tandems are offered in two to five standard sizes. Unless the captain is a foot or more taller than the stoker, one of these should fit. Expect to compromise a little at both ends. Typically, the captain may have to ride something a bit smaller than what he or she is used to, and the stoker may have to ride something a little bigger. Today's stout handlebar stems and long mountain bike seatposts can help bridge these gaps. In general, err on the side of a smaller frame, which is lighter and easier to stand over. Like with a single road bike, you want at least 2 inches of crotch clearance when both feet are on the ground.

There is no rule that says that the larger rider has to captain the bike, but you won't find a production tandem that allows the reverse. This is

Riding a tandem is a great way to get fit and enjoy the company of another rider.

because it takes upper-body strength to shift, brake, and pilot the big bike. Also, having the heavier rider in front means that your tandem will handle better and flex less. One more tip: A quick-release rear seatpost and adjustable rear stem will make it easy for you to ride with stokers of different sizes.

What gearing range and drivetrain equipment should we have? Tandems are like semi-trucks—slow going up hills and fast going down. Consequently, they need gearing that will span this range. Triple chainrings are standard. Here's an example for general road riding: 54/44/28-tooth chainrings and an 11T-to-28T cassette.

In the drivetrain department, Shimano and Campagnolo offer tandem riders a few crucial gifts such as brake/shift levers and bar-end levers. These are "indexed," allowing you to click precisely from gear to gear. They also help keep your hands on the bar while piloting the big bike, and all but eliminate fine-tuning after a shift.

Do we need a third brake? Most tandem makers offer a third brake (usually at the rear hub) in the form of a drum or disk. Choose this option if you frequently encounter long, steep descents or if you plan to carry a touring load or trailer. Generally, this brake is used in "drag" mode to temper speed so that you don't have to keep applying the rim brakes. It's usually operated with a ratcheted bar-end shifter. You can give your stoker control by putting it on the rear handlebar.

Besides the need for a hub that is threaded on the left side to accept the brake, you should also have 40 or 48 spokes to withstand the twisting load on the wheel.

What other special equipment do we need? You may want to have "dummy" brake levers in back to give the stoker an additional place to rest his or her hands. An extra-wide rear bar is standard to provide clearance for the captain's hips. Recessed cleat/pedal systems such as Shimano SPD allow the riders to put a foot down at stoplights without the risk of slipping. You should also carry a more extensive tool kit, including two tubes and extra-long tandem cables that you can never find in an emergency at Ralph's Bike & Mower.

To enhance stoker comfort, shock-absorbing seatposts are becoming a popular option. These can be added to any tandem. Also, several two-seaters are designed for a Softride suspension beam in back. This curved, carbon-composite cantilever eliminates the seatpost altogether. One end is bolted to the frame while the saddle attaches to the other end. The beam is free to flex continuously, sparing the stoker from road shock. Normal pedaling also makes it bob slightly, but most riders quickly adapt and stop noticing.

What tire pressure should we use? Tandems require high pressures because the combined rider weights can exceed 300 pounds. Otherwise, you may experience poor handling, rapid tire wear, and frequent pinch flats.

We won't recommend that you exceed the manufacturer's recommendation listed on the tire sidewall. But it's a fact that many tandem riders do. Even when using the listed maximum pressure, make sure that you have a tight-fitting rim/tire combination. (A tire that is easily removed without tools may blow off the rim at high pressure.) Here's a tip: When installing new tires, inflate them to max pressure and let the bike sit overnight to ensure that they won't blow off.

TANDEM TECHNIQUES

Nearly all aspects of piloting these big bikes are different from what you're used to with a single bike. But they are easy to master during the first few rides. Here are several tips for captains and stokers that will give you a head start.

Getting underway. Put the bike in a low gear on flat or slightly downhill terrain. With the stoker standing off to the side, lift a leg over the front handlebar, scissors-kick fashion, so that you're standing over the top tube. This is preferred to swinging a leg to the rear as you would on a single, because it's hard to clear the rear saddle and handlebar. Next, level the crankarms, right pedal forward. Put your foot into this pedal. Stabilize the bike, weight on your left foot on the ground, and have your stoker climb aboard and put both feet in the pedals. When the two of you are ready, push off with your left foot as you push down on the right pedal, and immediately begin pedaling. After a few strokes to gain momentum, coast if necessary so that you can get your left foot into the pedal correctly or cinch your toe straps.

Relaxing. Initially, you may feel that you are fighting each other, and that tremendous upper-body strength is required to stay upright. Ironically, if you quit battling this tension, your control will improve. Relax, keep your elbows bent, and avoid a death grip on the bar. The stoker must lean with the captain, being careful not to suddenly shift weight. (You will know you that are a team when you momentarily forget that you are not riding a single bike.)

Shifting. Switch gears often to maintain a normal 80-to-90-revolution-per-minute cadence. Unlike on a single, where you can stomp on the pedals a few times to get a slightly higher gear turning, a tandem's weight offers considerable resistance. Reach for the shifters often, or you will be reaching for aspirin later to numb your aching knees. This is why most tandems are 21 or 24 speeds. Also, shift to lower gears well in advance of steep hills. Even today's shift-under-pressure drivetrains will protest under full load when two engines are supplying the power.

Coming to a halt. When stopping momentarily, such as at a traffic light, the stoker can keep both feet in the pedals. The captain should support his (or her) partner by putting the right foot down and "sitting" on the top tube with the back of the left thigh. This provides enough stability to support even the heaviest rear rider and avoids additional fuss with pedals when it's time to restart.

Communication. Experienced tandem riders have an almost-telepathic knowledge of what their partners are about to do. Until you develop this, the captain will need to announce everything from shifting to taking a swig from a water bottle. For instance, as you approach a hill, call out the downshift. Likewise, stokers should inform the captain when sitting up to eat or put on a jacket. Since road shock is felt more acutely on tandems, the captain needs to announce unavoidable bumps and potholes, giving the stoker a chance to lift off the saddle slightly. For particularly bad sections, level the pedals, stand, and coast. Turns should be announced, too. In fact, the stoker should do the hand signaling.

Standing. Communication is also key to pedaling out of the saddle, something you can attempt after logging 100 miles or so. Standing isn't just a way to maintain speed over small rises; it's a crucial means to employ different muscle groups and avoid saddle soreness. Every tandem pair should practice it. Start in a parking lot. The captain shifts to the next smaller cog and announces his intention by calling, "Stand." Then, the next time the pedals come over the top, both riders rise simultaneously and apply power on the downstroke. Sway the bike slightly in rhythm with pedaling, as on a single, but keep the front wheel pointed straight ahead. The stoker should grasp the bar lightly and not try to muscle it. When he's ready, the captain should say, "Sit"—and down they go. With experience, the stoker will know it's time to sit based on the captain's body language, and no command will be necessary. Once you have mastered standing, do it often, whether the terrain warrants it or not. Your butts will thank you.

Descending. Gravity loves a tandem. This is why road models usually have a top gear of 54 × 12-tooth (54 × 12T), or higher. On descents keep in mind that the captain has the advantage of an unimpeded view. Initially, out of kindness to the stoker, be conservative. (A bumpy 45-mile-per-hour descent can be unnerving when all you can see is your partner's back.) Always err on the side of caution. Once a tandem begins to drift toward the road edge because you are going too fast through a curve, there's little hope of bringing it back. As mentioned above, add a third brake (hub or disk) if you ride in hill country.

Braking. On long descents pump the brakes instead of clamping them on the rim for long periods. This prevents overheating the pads and rims—dangerous because it reduces braking power and could cause a blowout. Better yet, apply drag with a third brake. Unlike when riding a single, in an emergency you can apply the more powerful front brake with abandon (as long as the pavement is free of sand or gravel). It's impossible to catapult yourself or your stoker over the bars.

Choosing a route. While screaming descents are fun, you'll find that a tandem is best suited to flat or rolling terrain, so choose routes accordingly. One of the most exhilarating things in cycling is jamming on a tandem in such conditions, staying on top of a big gear by standing to surmount small rises, then flying down the other side.

GLOSSARY

Aero bar: A handlebar that extends forward to allow a low, aerodynamic riding position with arms resting on padded supports. Aero extensions can be bolted to conventional drop handlebars.

Aerobic: Exercise that benefits the cardiovascular (heart and lungs) system. Also, an intensity of exercise below the level that produces lactic acid faster than the body can dispose of it. Oxygen needs are continuously met and the exercise can be continued for long periods.

Aerodynamic: A design of cycling equipment or a riding position that reduces wind resistance.

Anaerobic: An intensity of exercise past the point where the body can cope with its production of lactic acid and need for oxygen. Thus, the exercise level cannot be sustained for long.

Anaerobic threshold (AT): The point at which your muscle efficiency falls off significantly. It is at this point that your body's energy production switches from aerobic to anaerobic. Interval training raises the heart rate at which the threshold is crossed. Also called lactate threshold (LT).

Attack: An aggressive, high-speed acceleration away from other riders.

Blocking: Legally impeding the progress of riders in the pack to allow teammates a better chance of success.

Blow up: To suddenly be unable to continue at the required pace due to overexertion.

Bonk: A state of severe exhaustion caused by the depletion of the main source of fuel in the muscles. Once it occurs, there is no means of quick recovery.

Bottom bracket: The part of the frame where the crankset is installed.

Breakaway: A rider or group of riders who have escaped the pack.

Bridge, bridge a gap: To catch a rider or group that has opened a lead.

Bunch: The main cluster of riders in a race. Also called *group, pack, field,* and *peloton.*

Cadence: The rate of pedaling, measured in revolutions per minute (rpm) of one foot.

Captain: The front rider on a tandem bicycle.

Cassette: The set of gear cogs on the rear hub. Also called *freewheel, cluster,* or *block.*

Categories: The division of racers into groups based on ability and/or experience.

Century: A 100-mile ride.

Chainring: A sprocket attached to the right crankarm to drive the chain.

Chasers: Those who are trying to catch a group or a lead rider.

Chondromalacia: A serious knee injury in which there is disintegration of cartilage surfaces due to improper, sideways motion of the kneecap. Generally caused by weak quadriceps muscles. Symptoms include knee pain behind or on the side of the kneecap and a crunching sensation during bending.

Circuit: One loop of a road course that is ridden two or more times during a race.

Class: Something a talented pedaler is said to have.

Cleat: A metal or plastic fitting on the sole of a cycling shoe that engages the pedal.

Clinchers: Conventional tires with a separate inner tube.

Criterium: A mass-start race covering numerous laps of a course that is normally about 1 mile or less in length.

Cyclocross: A fall or winter event contested mostly or entirely off pavement. Courses include obstacles, steps, and steep hills that force riders to dismount and run with their bikes across their shoulders.

Domestique: A rider who sacrifices individual results to work for the team leaders.

Drafting: Riding closely behind another rider to take advantage of the windbreak (slipstream). Also called *sitting in* or *wheelsucking.*

Drivetrain: The components directly involved with making the rear wheel turn: the chain, crankset, and cassette. Also called *power train.*

Dropout: A slot in the frame into which the rear wheel axle fits.

Drops: The lower part of a down-turned handlebar typically found on a road bike. The curved portions are called the hooks.

Echelon: A form of paceline in which the riders angle off behind the leader to get maximum draft in a crosswind.

Ergometer: A stationary, bicycle-like device with adjustable pedal resistance used in physiological testing or for indoor training.

Fartlek: A Swedish word meaning "speed play," it is a training technique based on unstructured changes in pace and intensity. You alter your pace based on how you feel. It can be used instead of timed or measured intervals.

Field sprint: The dash for the finish line by the main group of riders.

Fixed gear: A direct-drive setup using one chainring and one rear cog, as on a track bike. When the rear wheel turns, so does the chain and crank; coasting isn't possible.

Full tuck: An extremely crouched position used for maximum speed on descents.

Gearing: The chain's position expressed as the number of teeth on the chainring and on the rear cog. Example: 53 × 16-tooth gear or simplified to 53 × 16T.

General classification: The overall standings in a stage race. Often referred to as GC.

Gorp: Good ol' raisins and peanuts, a high-energy mix to nibble on during rides. Can also include nuts, seeds, M&Ms, and granola.

Granny: Colloquial term for the tiny inner chainring on a triple chainring crankset.

Hammer: To ride hard and fast.

Hanging in: Barely maintaining contact at the back of the pack.

Headset: The parts at the top and bottom of the frame's head tube, into which the handlebar stem and fork are fitted.

Honking: Standing while climbing with hands on the brake lever hoods.

Intervals: A structured method of training that alternates relatively hard, short efforts with recovery periods of much easier riding.

Jam: A period of hard, fast riding.

Jump: A quick, hard acceleration.

Lactic acid: A by-product of anaerobic exercise that accumulates in the muscles, causing pain and fatigue.

Leadout: A race tactic in which a rider accelerates to his maximum speed for the benefit of a teammate in tow. The second rider then leaves the draft and sprints past at even greater speed near the finish line.

LSD: Long, steady distance. A training technique that requires a firm aerobic pace for at least 2 hours.

Mass start: Events such as road races and criteriums in which all contestants leave the starting line at the same time.

Maximum oxygen uptake (VO_2 max): The maximum amount of oxygen that a person can consume in 1 minute. It is basically determined by heredity and indicates potential performance in endurance sports.

Metric century: A 100-kilometer ride (62 miles).

Minuteman: In a time trial the rider who is one place in front of you in the starting order. So called because in most time trials, riders start on 1-minute intervals.

Motorpace: Riding behind a motorcycle or other vehicle that breaks the wind.

Mudguards: Fenders.

NORBA: National Off-Road Bicycle Association, the governing body of off-road racing in America. A division of USA Cycling.

Off the back: Describes one or more riders who had failed to keep pace with the main group. Sometimes referred to as OTB.

Orthotics: Custom-made supports worn in shoes to help neutralize biomechanical imbalances in the feet or legs.

Overgear: Using a gear ratio too big for the terrain or level of fitness.

Overtraining: Deep-seated fatigue, both physical and mental, caused by training at a volume higher than that to which the body can adapt.

Oxygen debt: The amount of oxygen that needs to be consumed to pay back the deficit incurred by anaerobic work.

Paceline: A group formation in which each rider takes a turn breaking the wind at the front before pulling off, dropping to the rear position, and riding the others' draft until at the front once again.

Peak: A relatively short period during which maximum performance is achieved.

Peloton: The main group of riders in a race.

Prime: A special award given to the leader on selected laps during a criterium or the first rider to reach a certain landmark in a road race. It's used to heighten the action. Pronounced "preem."

Pull, pull through: Take a turn at the front.

Pull off: To move to the side after riding in the lead so that another rider can come to the front.

Pusher: A rider who pedals in a large gear at a relatively slow cadence, relying on the gear size for speed.

Quadriceps: The large muscle in front of the thigh, the strength of which helps determine a cyclist's ability to pedal with power.

Recumbent: A bicycle on which the rider is in a reclining, feet-first position.

Road bike: A bicycle with a freewheel, derailleurs, and brakes.

Road race: A mass-start race that goes from point to point, covers one large loop or is held on a circuit longer than those used for criteriums.

Road rash: Any skin abrasion resulting from a fall.

Rollers: An indoor training device that works like a treadmill for bikes.

Saddle sores: Skin problems in the crotch that develop from chafing caused by pedaling action. Sores can range from tender raw spots to boil-like lesions if infection occurs.

Saddle time: Time spent cycling.

Sag wagon: A motor vehicle that follows a group of riders, carrying equipment and lending assistance in the event of difficulty. Also called *broom wagon.*

Sit on a wheel: To ride in someone's draft.

Slingshot: To sprint around another rider after taking advantage of their draft.

Slipstream: The pocket of calmer air behind a moving rider. Also called the draft.

Snap: The ability to accelerate quickly.

Soft-pedal: To rotate the pedals without actually applying power.

Speedwork: Fast training using techniques like intervals, sprints, time trials, and motorpacing.

Spin: To pedal at high cadence.

Spinner: A rider who pedals in a moderate gear at a relatively fast cadence, relying on pedal revolutions per minute for speed.

Squirrel: A nervous or unstable rider who can't be trusted to maintain a steady line.

Stage race: A multi-day event consisting of point-to-point and circuit road races, time trials, and, sometimes, criteriums. The winner is the rider with the lowest elapsed time for all stages.

Stoker: The rear rider on a tandem bicycle.

Straight block: A cassette with cogs that increase in size in one-tooth increments.

Suppleness: A quality of highly conditioned leg muscles that allows a rider to pedal at high cadence with smoothness and power. Also known by the French term *souplesse*.

Take a flyer: To suddenly sprint away from a group.

Tandem: A bicycle that has seats, bars, and pedals for two or more riders, one behind the other.

Team time trial (TTT): A race against the clock with two or more riders working together.

Tempo: Fast riding at a brisk cadence.

Throw the bike: A racing technique in which a rider pushes the bike ahead of his or her body at the finish line, gaining several inches in hopes of winning a close sprint.

Time trial (TT): A race against the clock in which individual riders start at set intervals and cannot give or receive a draft.

Tops: The part of a drop handlebar between the stem and the brake levers.

Training effect: The result of exercise done with an intensity and duration sufficient to bring about positive physiological changes.

Tubular: A lightweight tire that has the tube permanently sewn inside the casing. Also called a sew-up. The tire is glued to the rim.

Turkey: An unskilled cyclist.

Turnaround: The point where the riders reverse direction on an out-and-back time trial course.

UCI: Union Cycliste Internationale, the world governing body of bicycle racing, headquartered in Geneva, Switzerland.

USA Cycling: The umbrella organization for U.S. bicycle racing. Affiliated with the UCI.

USCF: U.S. Cycling Federation, the organization that governs amateur road and track racing in America. A division of USA Cycling.

USPRO: U.S. Professional Racing Organization, the organization in charge of professional bicycle racing in America. A division of USA Cycling.

Velodrome: A banked track for bicycle racing.

Wheelsucker: Someone who drafts behind others and doesn't take a pull.

Wind up: Steady acceleration to an all-out effort.

ABOUT THE AUTHORS

John Allen is an expert on the traffic skills required for urban cycling. A former contributing editor with Bicycling magazine, he now works as a consultant in lawsuits involving bicycle accidents.

Arnie Baker, M.D., is an advisory board member for Bicycling magazine and a several-time masters champion. He is also author of Smart Cycling.

Edmund R. Burke, Ph.D., is an exercise physiologist who has worked with the U.S. national cycling team since the mid-1970s. He was director of Project 96, American cycling's elite training and technology program for the Atlanta Olympics. He's also the author of several books on high-level cycling performance.

Geoff Drake, Bicycling magazine's editor, is a veteran road racer and journalist who is also a licensed cycling coach. His personal training regimen has included towing daughter Andrea for thousands of miles in his bike trailer.

Jim Langley, a master mechanic, is Bicycling magazine's technical editor and new products coordinator. For several years he managed one of northern California's premier bike shops.

Gary Legwold is a freelance writer with expertise in cycling. His forte is making complex issues understandable and interesting, as he does in chapter 42.

Fred Matheny, Bicycling magazine's training and fitness editor, has been racing his road bike for more than 20 years. In 1996, he was a member of *Bicycling's* record-breaking senior relay team in the Race Across America, riding from Los Angeles to Savannah in 5 days and 11 hours. Fred is the author of three books, including *Bicycling Magazine's Complete Guide to Riding and Racing Techniques.*

Michael McGettigan is a bicycling writer and advocate who has survived three decades of cycling in such places as Philadelphia, New York City, and Barcelona.

Rory O'Reilly, a former Olympic cyclist and national track champion, has set two world track records. He lives in California, where he still competes and coaches.

Jo Ostgarden is a freelance writer who enjoys assignments dealing with nutrition and cycling performance. She is a long-distance rider who lives in the Pacific Northwest.

Robert M. Otto, Ph.D., is a triathlete and director of the human performance laboratory at Adelphi University in Garden City, New York.

Ed Pavelka has been riding the road for fun, fitness, and competition since the mid-1970s. His professional writing career includes 18 cycling books. He was *Bicycling's* executive editor for 10 years and now serves as the magazine's director of New Ventures.

Nelson Pena, formerly a senior editor at *Bicycling* magazine, where he wrote the popular "New Cyclist" column, is publisher of *Mountain Bike* magazine.

Davis Phinney, a 1984 Olympian, won 328 events in his career—more than any American road racer ever. Two of these victories came in Tour de France stages. Now living in Colorado with his wife, Connie Carpenter (1984 Olympic road champion), and their two sons, Davis is a contributing editor for *Bicycling* magazine, works as a TV commentator, and directs the Carpenter-Phinney Cycling Camps.

Julie Walsh, M.S., R.D., is a triathlete and nutritionist who frequently writes for *Bicycling.* She lives in New York City, where she often can be found swimming in the waters surrounding Manhattan and riding with the Century Road Club Association.

PHOTO CREDITS

Donna Chiarelli: pages 61, 139

John Hamel: pages 8, 9, 10

Robert Houser: pages 36, 47

John Karapelou: pages 169, 176

Mel Lindstrom: pages 15, 16, 17, 18, 19

Scott Markewitz: page 3

Hughes Martin: page 123

Mike Shaw: page 30

Graham Watson: page 116

INDEX

Underscored page references indicate boxed text. **Boldface** references indicate illustrations.

Z